UNIVERSITY OF WINNIPEG
LIBRARY
515 Portage Avenue
Winnipeg, Manitoba R3B 2E9

The First Student Movement

*Plus ça change,
plus c'est la même chose.*

Kennikat Press
National University Publications
Series in Political Science

THE FIRST STUDENT MOVEMENT

Student Activism in the United States During the 1930s

RALPH S. BRAX

National University Publications
KENNIKAT PRESS // 1981
Port Washington, N.Y. // London

For My Parents
and Sue

Copyright © 1981 by Kennikat Press Corp. All rights reserved. No part of this publication may be reproduced, stored in a retrieval system, or transmitted, in any form or by any means, electronic, mechanical, photocopying, recording, or otherwise, without the prior written permission of the publisher.

Manufactured in the United States of America

Published by
Kennikat Press Corp.
Port Washington, N.Y. / London

Library of Congress Cataloging in Publication Data

Brax, Ralph S   1944-
   The first student movement.

   (National university publications)
   Bibliography: p.
   Includes index.
   1. Student movements—United States. I. Title.
LA229.B63   378'.1981'0973   80-18888
ISBN 0-8046-9266-1

CONTENTS

1. STUDENT ATTITUDES   3
2. THE BEGINNING YEARS, 1930-1933   18
3. ACTIVISM, PROTEST, AND CONFLICT: The Student Movement Comes of Age, 1934-1936   36
4. THE ACTIVISTS AND THEIR LEADERS: Analyzing the Issues   54
5. THE INSTITUTIONAL SIDE   62
6. ISOLATIONISM VERSUS COLLECTIVE SECURITY   78
7. THE MOVEMENT ENDS, 1939-1941   90
8. REFLECTIONS AND CONCLUSIONS   104
    BIBLIOGRAPHY   110
    INDEX   117

The First Student Movement

ABOUT THE AUTHOR

Dr. Ralph S. Brax is a professor of history at Antelope Valley College in Lancaster, California. He is the author of "When Students First Organized Against War" in the *New York Historical Society Quarterly*.

1

STUDENT ATTITUDES

Although the first nationally organized student movement in America occurred in the 1930s, student opposition to the established order has had a long tradition. The history of protest within and against American colleges and universities is nearly as old as the institutions themselves. While most undergraduates have tended to be inactive and passive, they have had periods of sudden and explosive activity. From the earliest days, college students in the United States have rebelled against what they considered repressive authority and unrepresentative administrations. As one study concluded, "Student activism is as American as apple pie." (Ellsworth, p. 5.)

The first recorded rebellion occurred in 1766 at Harvard University, over the poor quality of butter served in the commons. The rallying call of the protestors was, "Behold our Butter stinketh." Other demonstrations at Harvard followed in 1768, 1780, and 1805. According to the historian Samuel Eliot Morison, the typical student of the late eighteenth century was "an atheist in religion, an experimentalist in morals, a rebel in authority." The authority against which the student rebelled, however, was only collegiate.

Few student disturbances in the nineteenth century had an ideological basis or were concerned with national politics. Undergraduates engaged in protests which involved specific disagreements directed against fellow students, professors, or university administrations. Often student unrest took the form of Town versus Gown. Between 1800 and 1850, Harvard, Yale, Princeton, Brown, Dartmouth, South Carolina, Amherst, and Vermont all experienced at least one organized student revolt.

At Princeton between 1800 and 1830, six violent demonstrations occurred. During one riot, students took possession of several buildings and defied the authorities to try and enter. At Brown, "deliberate, organized, and protracted" rebellions between 1824 and 1826 forced the president to resign. Needless to say, the administrators of these schools took a dim view of what was happening. John Wheelock, president of Dartmouth, observed, "Melancholy must be the prospect...of our country, when students...undertake to insult humanity and justice, to prostrate the laws and overturn the social order."

One illustration of the Town-and-Gown clashes that occurred in the nineteenth century was the battle that raged during May 1842 between the students of Harvard and the working people of Cambridge and Boston. The workers objected to the Oxford caps worn by the students, and began wearing large imitation hats to display their resentment. The undergraduates, however, failed to see the humor in this, and started knocking the caps off the heads of the workers. Before the controversy ended, a throng of three hundred "truckmen" and "rowdies" battled fifty students, who were armed with "daggers, pokers, . . . and clubs." Although it was a minor incident, the conflict revealed the latent class tension that existed between the elitist students and the townspeople of Cambridge and Boston, a situation that was commonplace in many college towns and cities.

Although in the nineteenth century most student protest movements were nonideological in nature, one was not. Beginning in 1833, antislavery or abolitionist student groups began appearing on college campuses. The first such group was formed at Amherst. It started slowly, but a year later, one-fourth of the college's enrollment had joined the "Auxiliary Anti-Slavery Society." In the fall of 1834, the president of Amherst, Herman Humphrey, urged the students to disband, stating it would be for their "own best good." The students resisted; Humphrey and the faculty moved to suppress the group; and by March 1835 the society had been dissolved.

At Lane Theological Seminary in Cincinnati, Ohio, activists, having been notified that the school's trustees had ordered their abolitionist group to disband, renounced the decision and seceded to Oberlin College, where they became known as the Rebels. At the University of Michigan, an abolitionist club, organized in the late 1830s, was devoted to smuggling runaway slaves into Canada. Other schools with antislavery societies included Williams, Illinois, Bowdoin, Dartmouth, New York, and Miami University (Ohio).

Between 1870 and 1900, numerous student demonstrations occurred across the country. Most involved one of two themes—either they were protests aimed at the doctrine of *in loco parentis* (colleges which governed student behavior as sternly as parents) or they were attempts to remove unpopular college presidents. The student newspaper at Williams College, the *Argo*, declared, "Few parents would attempt any such government of twenty-year-olds as do colleges of their students." The entire student body of Middlebury College, in Vermont, went on strike in the fall of 1879, and desisted only after the trustees installed a new president. In 1885 at the University of California, Berkeley, enraged students thrust a ladder through the front window of the president's house. Shortly thereafter, he resigned his post.

More localized than the student revolts of the 1930s and involving far fewer students, campus disturbances in the nineteenth century were not part of a single organized protest movement. Most activists were not interested in changing the nature of society and possessed no real political or ideological differences with their teachers and administration officials. As one observer has concluded, students "accepted the society as it was, and looked forward . . . to becoming its leaders." (Feuer, p. 335.)

What little student political activism that existed during the early years of the twentieth century was channeled into settlement work. Thousands of students and young graduates took up the cause of helping the newly arrived immigrants and urban poor. By 1911, more than ten thousand students were working in twenty-five hundred settlement houses. One author has written that settlements were "protests by students against learning that was never put to use." (Peterson, p. 184.)

The campus scene in the 1920s was quiescent, although there were occasional flare-ups. A few antiwar Progressive and Socialist student clubs appeared, as activists "demanded to hear all sides of every question." In addition, on various campuses underground student papers sprang up: the *Gadfly* at Harvard, the *Critic* at Oberlin, the *Tempest* at Michigan, and the *Proletarian* at Wisconsin. The *New Student,* the periodical of the Intercollegiate Liberal League, was the predominant expression of student activism in the twenties. In presenting the magazine's point of view, its editor, Douglas Haskell, declared, "With all respect to the older generation, some of us become more and more certain that they cannot feel the chaos as we do. . . . Spiritually, this is an age of ruin—of nausea. . . . Mechanization must go."

The decade of the 1920s, however, was basically a conservative time for college students as it was for most Americans. A presidential straw vote conducted in 120 colleges and universities in 1924 revealed that a larger percentage of students supported President Calvin Coolidge than did the actual voters (59 percent to 54 percent), and fewer undergraduates voted for Robert LaFollette, the Progressive party candidate, than did the nation as a whole (14 percent to 16 percent). One study of campus life observed that the twenties were dominated by the "rah-rah college boy and girl," and concluded that it was an era of "fun, self-indulgence, and optimism." (Lee, pp. 43, 47.) In the 1930s, however, the ramifications of the Depression and the rumblings of war would produce and sustain a decade of student activism of a scope and intensity previously unknown to American society.

Although the available sociological and psychological data is sparse and fugitive, one is able to construct a portrait of the student of the thirties. While the economic status of the student's family, his or her race and intelligence, and the number of students enrolled in the college remained relatively unchanged, some critical variations did occur in the life style and outlook of most undergraduates. Evidence suggests that college students continued to be conservative and traditional in their sexual activities and moral beliefs and in the sophistication of their political attitudes. Many of their ideas and beliefs, however, were changing from those held by undergraduates prior to the Depression, especially their views of college, of the purpose of government, and of the role of the United States in world affairs.

The standard description of college life following the First World War intimates a revolution in student morals, behavior, and manners, a total rejection of long-accepted mores. Agreeing with this position, a recent study by Seymour M. Lipset and Gerald M. Schaflander states that this revolution was "evidenced by new dress styles, the open flaunting of sex and liquor, and the strong objections voiced to conventional religion." The findings of Alfred Kinsey, the noted American chronicler of human sexual behavior, that women were freer sexually is usually given as the crucial corroboration.

While this conventional assumption overstates the change that was taking place, a liberalizing movement was occurring in regard to student attitudes and behavior toward morality, sex, and manners. In 1933, Alzada Comstock, a professor of economics at Mount Holyoke College, described what she considered to be the much-changed woman undergraduate. While on campus, this new female student wore "black and white sport shoes, . . . a dress which was meant for the tennis court, . . . and one of those flapping brown coats." But when she went out on the town, "she [was] smartly dressed from the peak of her little hat, tilted over one eye, to those fragile matching shoes which click so briskly on the pavement." Alzada Comstock concluded that the woman college student of the thirties was "unrecognizably tidy."

A survey of male student opinion of this "new feminine attire" indicates that most were against it. It was reported, at the University of California, Los Angeles, for example, that there existed, "a unanimous razzberry for girls who wear wide-brimmed hats to a dance." A sizable majority voted eagerly for the return of "the sweater and skirt appearance" on campus, with a "snug, small-brimmed hat," and the men stated their preference for simple evening wear with a minimum of jewelry and bows. Toward the end of the decade, the skirt and sweater resurfaced, with blue jeans also appearing. Bobbed hair was on the decline, replaced with the shoulder-length pageboy.

Professor Comstock also observed that women students were no longer isolated on campus. Now, during the thirties, "from the set of sun as far into the night as the local curfew permits, a women's college campus is thick with young men who have arrived in open cars from anywhere within a radius of a hundred miles." In late 1931, the president of the University of Wyoming, A. G. Crane, personally conducted a campaign to stop these "modern indulgences" on the part of his students. The high point of his efforts came when he spied on parked cars to secure evidence "of alleged necking and petting" on campus. As a result of his clandestine activities and subsequent announcement of having witnessed student misconduct, a twenty-four-hour strike was called by the student body.

The concern over changed sexual behavior was not restricted to the University of Wyoming. The president of the University of Detroit ordered women students not to converse with men. The edict was designed "to keep girls from love-making in college so that they may devote more time to study." At Oregon State University, officials in an effort to curb increased sexual activity banned the presence of automobiles on campus. College administrators argued that such vehicles posed "an environment favorable to petting." The school newspaper, the *Barometer*, reported that there were few arrests as the campus police seemed reluctant to cite students found driving cars. Sterner opposition came from the city leaders and businessmen who disliked the ban because it interfered with retail income and caused unemployment.

In 1923, more than three thousand college students were asked a set of questions regarding their attitudes toward a variety of social and personal issues. Ten years later, in 1933, the test was again given to approximately the same number of students. The researcher, Walter Buck, concluded that the second test showed "a consistent liberalizing of opinion." Undergraduates in 1933 disapproved of far fewer ideas and activities, including such behavior as smoking, gambling, flirting, immodesty, and divorce. A similar study conducted in 1934 discovered that college students in overwhelming numbers indicated they did not consider sex to be "dirty and shameful," or divorce to be "wrong." The number of students expressing these "liberal" opinions had doubled between 1928, when the test was first given, and 1934.

Doctor Nicholas Murray Butler, the president of Columbia University, in reviewing the state of America's youth in the early 1930s, was upset by what he observed. He asserted that "present-day habits as manifested in every sort of public place . . . are time and again quite shocking." He concluded that "carelessness and inconsiderateness in dress, in speech, and in personal habits have become all too common . . . among the younger generation." He felt that the college student of the 1930s showed an "unconcern for standards of excellence and an overconcern for the quick satisfaction of their own immediate conveniences and desires." (*Spectator*, September 27, 1934.)

Although a liberalizing trend was evident, and several university presidents exhibited some serious handwringing over the situation, it appears that most students still possessed traditional sexual and moral beliefs. A study by George J. Dudycha, involving over 1,150 college freshmen and seniors, indicates that the large majority continued to hold conventional moral views. The statement that ranked highest in belief for all students—a 97 percent acceptance—was, "It is one's duty to lead a clean personal life." Over 80 percent of the students also agreed that it was wrong for unmarried couples to live together, or for anyone to have "promiscuous sexual relations." Three-fourths of those tested believed it was wrong for men and women—more so for women than men—to use profane language and to consume alcohol. It is important to note the striking similarities in the answers for both freshmen and seniors, indicating that college life had little effect on changing moral values.

In 1937, the *Stanford Daily* distributed a questionnaire to determine the sexual activities of the student body. While the majority of both men and women undergraduates responding admitted that they "necked," most women asserted they did not "pet" or kiss on the first date, and the majority of men declared they thought less of women "who let you kiss them on your first date" and wanted their wives to "have had no previous sex experience." An extensive poll conducted by *Fortune* magazine found that most young people believed marriage was the best of human institutions. It further reported that sixty percent of college women and fifty percent of college men wanted to marry within a year or two of graduation, and about fifty percent of both sexes hoped for children soon after marriage.

Maxine Davis, who traveled throughout the United States and interviewed hundreds of undergraduates during the 1930s concluded that in regard to matters of sex, nearly everyone believed it was "right and decent to have intimate relations with the person you love," but that one should avoid promiscuity, which students considered to be "cheap, vulgar, and immoral." In 1936, in response to the question of whether divorce should be made easier to obtain, a Gallup poll showed that 75 percent of the "college students" answered no, thus placing them within the mainstream of American popular opinion.

As an example of how traditional student attitudes were concerning sex, the American Student Union—a leftist student political organization—broke new ground in 1936 by publishing a series of articles on "sex education," and yet the "message" in those articles was quite conservative. Dr. Marie Warner, the author of the series, declared that the "most complete and satisfying response of the sexual impulse is obtained through marriage, when a permanent, monogamous sex relationship exists." In the correspondence section, a college girl asked the psychologist what she should do to help solve her problem of wanting to "resort to petting." The good doctor reassured her that she was "a perfectly normal individual," and that she ought to try "to find an outlet in dancing, club activities and out-door recreation." If the feeling persisted, she suggested that the troubled girl should take "a sedative in the form of Triple Bromide pills, grade 15, twice a day for a period of three weeks," which Dr. Warner believed might quiet the restlessness and physical urge. (*Student Advocate*, October-November 1936, pp. 16-17.)

One of the changes in campus life styles was student drinking habits, as the consumption of alcohol on the part of both sexes was on the rise in most colleges throughout the decade. At the University of Minnesota, officials became so concerned with the problem that they called in federal authorities "to drive the bootleggers from the campus and curb student drinking." As a result, on March 12, 1931, five persons were arrested and four student "establishments" were closed.

At the University of Michigan, evidence not only suggested that students were drinking more, but Robert Clancy, a Congressman from Ann Arbor, reported that some students were "selling liquor to pay their way through school." The editors of the *Daily Bruin*, the student newspaper at the University of California, Los Angeles, concluded that "drinking is a serious situation on every campus," and added that "it will exist until the question of national prohibition has been solved." After repeal, during the fall of 1934, beer was introduced in the dormitory dining halls at Columbia University. It seemed to catch on immediately with reports that "one out of every five students are drinking a stein of beer a day." The *Alumni News*, which did not appreciate the innovation, pointed out that many of the students had already suggested that "different brands of brew be tried," and that many of the student waiters had learned how "to tap a keg quite gracefully."

Two studies completed in 1937 effectively illustrate student attitudes and behavior toward alcohol. The *Literary Digest* sent questionnaires to hundreds of college presidents and undergraduate editors requesting their comments on the drinking situation in their respective institutions. The replies, which were received from more than 550 colleges, indicated to the authors of the study that student drinking was on the increase everywhere. Nearly every undergraduate student editor reported on the plentiful use of "hard and light intoxicants," and the information also showed that "women students have lost their moral revulsion against drinking."

Arnold Lerner, who was then editor of the *Campus* at City College of New York, declared that the students whom he observed "pride themselves on their ability to drink anything, anywhere, and at any time." The undergraduate editor at Mount Holyoke reported that there was "more drinking on dates during the week" than formerly, and editor W. T. Hunt at Purdue estimated that there was "a 500 percent increase in drinking [since] 1933." The *Literary Digest* summarized that the larger the college and the higher its academic standing, "the fewer its regulations and the less the observance."

A study by Paul Studenski, involving the drinking habits of more than twenty-three hundred college students in New York City, reveals that 83 percent drank regularly or occasionally, the women students ranking proportionally as high as men in the number of imbibers. Researchers also found that approximately a fifth of the men consumed three or more glasses of hard liquor a week, while one-half of them drank more than three glasses of beer a week. Women had similar tastes, with the exception of their dislike for beer. The reasons given by most students as to why they drank were, "It makes one gayer" and "Others do it."

Placing student drinking habits in perhaps a more realistic perspective, the editors of the *Occident*, a student journal at the University of California, Berkeley, believed that while many collegians were "reverting to more intemperate habits," they nevertheless were drinking in moderation and "doing it sanely." They observed that students "piece out intervals between their alcoholic bouts with good homemade beer, and no matter what the occasion, rarely pass out." They concluded that the "hard drinker is rapidly disappearing from the campus," and that most students did not get drunk more than once or twice a semester.

Life styles on many college campuses changed as a significant number of students, because of the depressed economy, began living in student-owned and -operated dormitories. Those undergraduates who could not or did not want to live at home, and were unable to pay the rents charged by college residence halls or fraternities and sororities, often formed associations, or "cooperatives," to reduce the cost of living. Renting an empty dormitory, fraternity, or a large house in the neighborhood, these students would offer room and board at a minimal rate and require that all residing there do the chores necessary to make the communal arrangement a success.

At Texas A & M in 1932, twelve students repaired an old haunted house and proceeded to live there. The following year, more than one hundred students were living there in ten cooperative units. At the University of Idaho, a cooperative began in 1932 and furnished room and board for 350 students for $140 a year. That same year at the University of Michigan, the Socialist Club organized a cooperative house to accommodate thirty students at the rate of two dollars a day for room and board, with each member required to work a given number of hours each week. The furniture, beds, and such, for the house were donated by sympathetic faculty members and Ann Arbor residents.

The cooperative idea caught on early and continued throughout the decade. By 1938, student-run dormitories could be found on more than a hundred campuses, involving over 70,000 students. Moreover, such cooperative associations became involved not only with housing, but spread into such other areas as book and supply stores, restaurants, and planned vacations. At the University of Washington in 1937, for example, the student cooperative ran several stores, cafeterias, and eight boardinghouses solely for its members. A cooperative lunchroom was organized at the University of Oregon, where three meals a day were served for $2.50 a week. It was estimated that in various colleges, 160 cooperative bookstores, laundries, general stores, dormitories, and cafeterias did an annual business of $3,000,000.

Along with the popularity of cooperative dormitories, the 1930s witnessed a large amount of opposition from college students to fraternities and sororities. Attitudinal studies, done in 1925, 1928, and repeated in 1934, show that by 1934 students had become disenchanted with fraternities. The results indicate that the overwhelming majority of students in the thirties had discarded the belief that "fraternities are desirable."

A student from Albion College in Michigan reflected the view of many when he declared that the only men who joined fraternities were those "filled with the egotism of high school social success, . . . and whose environment has denied them social relationships." At Columbia University in 1933, the *Spectator*, the college newspaper, called for the abolition of all the fraternities on campus. The primary reason was that the *Spectator* had discovered that the fraternities had "auctioned off" many of their honorary positions to the highest bidder. In the spring elections of 1934, the fraternities lost control of undergraduate government at Columbia for the first time in decades, as a "strong independent machine" won a majority of student council offices. Fraternity members had every right to be concerned, since one of the main planks of the independents was the abolition of the fraternity system.

On the West Coast, the criticism of fraternities was also heavy. At the University of California, Berkeley, a student maintained that fraternities attracted "athletes, boomers, and loafers in large numbers." His conclusion was that the school's image had suffered "due to fraternity members' peculiar and childish practices and pranks." At the University of California, Los Angeles, the *Daily Bruin* declared in horror that in all likelihood the college would have, in a few more years, "as many fraternities as there are at Berkeley." It urged that something be done immediately to prevent this from occurring, declaring, "The right time to act is before the situation becomes unbearable."

As an indication of how deep sentiment ran against what fraternities stood for, the editors of the *Student*, the undergraduate newspaper at the University of Missouri, advocated the abolition of both fraternities and the annual "Homecoming" celebration, which was sponsored by the fraternity council. According to the editors, the cherished tradition of returning to the campus had become "an affair of debauchery and moral filth." The event involved, they declared, nothing more than hundreds of alumni returning to the university "bottle-laden, staggering, and insensible to the real meaning of homecoming." The returning alumni, they ended, were simply "a drunken mob."

All the commentators and analysts of various aspects of student life during the 1930s virtually agree that a more sober and serious mood became evident on college campuses, as the Depression ended the carefree days of the twenties, with students enrolling in more economics and social-science courses and showing a greater interest in the political happenings of the day. In 1935, the annual report of the Carnegie Foundation, for example, concluded that the "student on the campus is no longer the blasé, sophisticated student of the twenties; he is a hard-working, serious-minded person who demands more of the college library . . . and the instructor than did his brother of a decade ago."

Undergraduate editors from colleges and universities across the country also stated that the college student of the 1930s had become more solemn. D. B. Hardeman, editor of the *Daily Texan*, the student publication at the University of Texas, emphasized that "the rah-rah days of the twenties are gone." He argued that the "greater use of libraries, the increased interest of students in politics, . . . and the de-emphasis on fraternities and athletics, . . . show the college man is thinking more and playing less." Chandler Harris, when he was editor of the *Daily Bruin*, stated, "The depression killed Joe College. Economic necessity has forced thought into the life of college students." At the University of Chicago, the editor of the *Daily Maroon* observed a new trend "toward political and international discussion by students." And at Columbia, Arnold Beichman, editor of the *Spectator*, declared that while the 1920s witnessed "the athletic do-or-die spirit which the columns of a college newspaper gushed forth," in 1933, "we read quiet, logical criticism and discuss matters which past generations of undergraduates might have resented."

This new sense of purpose is also reflected in the types of courses students selected and in attitudinal studies done at the time. Beginning in 1935, undergraduate students at Harvard were given a choice of various elective courses. The largest gains in enrollment occurred in the introductory courses in economics and in government. Such popular classes as those in music and art, suffered a reduction in size. As one faculty member remarked, "No professor of economics is now surprised to be waited upon by a student committee requesting a public lecture, . . . nor is he surprised to see the lecture well attended."

A 1934 study by Dorothy H. Yates of 239 students at San Jose State College reveals that approximately 85 percent of them believed that the Depression had "made them more serious in their thinking." One girl undergraduate replied that the economic troubles of the day had forced her to "snap out of a high school attitude toward life, become more serious, and wonder what things are all about." The study showed that 70 percent of the students were deeply interested in the problems of the country. Another study by Nettie P. McGill and Ellen N. Matthews, analyzing what type of leisure-time activities most college students and young people in New York participated in, discovered that a high proportion of the state's youth did not engage in any leisure-time activities. Three-fourths of the young people whom researchers questioned had never visited a museum or art gallery, nor attended a concert for over a year; one-half of them had not gone to a dance, taken a walk for pleasure, or driven a car in at least a year. Practically negligible was the number of students who had engaged in any "civic, political, or philanthropic activities."

Not only had most students become more serious about their college studies and their outlook toward life in general, but the 1930s also brought a shift in the political outlook of students, with most of the evidence indicating that undergraduates had become far more liberal in their attitudes toward the role of government in society and in many of their social and economic ideas. A prominent student journal declared in July 1932 that "a new student has arisen." It asserted that the Depression was "the teacher of new values" that characterized this changed undergraduate. It concluded that "today's student is breaking thru [sic] the old, narrow-fitting academic bonds. His school-fed illusions are fading away. He is beginning to realize that his life is inextricably bound up with the social system under which he lives." (*Student Review*, p. 3.)

Throughout the 1930s a number of studies were conducted at various universities to determine the political attitudes of students. The great majority of these tests found that students were moving leftward. E. L. Breemes, H. H. Remmers, and C. L. Morgan, researchers at Purdue University, administered such studies yearly during the entire decade. Their results indicate a significant trend toward a more liberal viewpoint for both men and women during the middle and later years of the 1930s. The greatest liberality was expressed toward such issues as government ownership of railroads, favorable legislation to farmers, and heavy taxation of large fortunes.

In 1934, a test was given to more than seven hundred students attending Kansas State Teachers College to determine whether they were liberal or conservative. The crucial finding by W. J. Boldt and J. B. Stroud was that 65 percent of all the responses from this small, rural Kansas college were liberal ones. Three-fifths of the students agreed that "educational forces should be directed toward a more socialistic order of society." Eighty-five percent contended that huge fortunes in America "endanger democracy," and 70 percent felt that "many more industries . . . should be owned and operated by the workers themselves." A study of Maryland students by Howard M. Bell shows that the great majority believed the role and agenda of the federal government should be increased. Nearly 75 percent of the students felt it was the government's job to regulate hours and wages, and 90 percent agreed that the problem of relief should be solved by the government rather than by individuals.

In 1929, a test was administered by Gardner Murphy and Rensis Likert to more than 170 students from Michigan and Columbia universities to measure their attitudes toward a variety of domestic and foreign issues. In 1934, the same test was again given to a large number of those who had been in the original sample. The results indicated a shift toward a more radical direction in every area tested. One student, whose liberalism had increased, felt it was because "events in Europe showed me the ineffectiveness of minor reform and compromise." A second student, who had been a "strong Republican" in 1929, favored a "socialist form of government" because he had heard Norman Thomas speak; and yet another student had veered to the Left because he had read *The Education of Henry Adams*. The student whose views had shifted the most—from very conservative to extremely liberal—believed the reasons were, "The depression; difficulty of finding a decent job; and Roosevelt being such a powerful figure."

A 1934 study by Theodore B. Brameld of over 850 students from nine eastern colleges and universities concluded that a majority of them were either quite liberal or radical in many of their social and political views.

The responses also indicated, however, that many students were inconsistent or confused in their beliefs. Of the fifty propositions to which they were asked to state the degree of their commitment, the one receiving the greatest amount of allegiance was, "Wealth should be much more equally distributed." Moreover, a large majority agreed that future depressions would result "if capitalism continues," and that "all electric power should be owned by the government." Nevertheless, while most students felt that unemployment was not decreasing, they also stated that "another era of prosperity is rapidly approaching." And while 50 percent agreed that Socialism was "an experiment worth trying," only 13 percent thought that a communist society was preferable to a capitalist one. In all, revolutionary suggestions were overwhelmingly rejected, as most believed that the Roosevelt administration's recovery programs should not be opposed.

Although a number of different reasons have been offered to explain why the students expressed such liberal political and social attitudes, nearly all researchers agree that the undergraduates' liberalism increased between the freshman and senior years. Theodore Newcomb, in his study of Bennington students during the late 1930s, found that nearly all left college considerably more liberal than they were when they entered as freshmen. Another researcher concluded, "Freshmen are by several degrees the most conservative of all students tested." And C. Michael Stanton, the author of a recent analysis of various surveys of student political attitudes during the thirties, has remarked that "students expressed more liberal views toward economic planning than their counterparts before the depression, and this liberalism increased during the four years of college attendance." (Lipset and Schaflander, pp. 178-79.)

While most of the evidence shows students moving to the Left during the 1930s, some does not. A committee of the American Association of University Professors conducted a study to determine the effect of the Depression on higher education. The only area for which there was so little data available that the researchers were unable to reach any conclusions was the question of the economy's effect on student attitudes and ideologies. Its advice was to scrutinize the statements that had been made "concerning the effect of the depression upon student thought and action."

In a nationwide college poll taken in the fall of 1932, the choice of most students to be the next President of the United States was Herbert Hoover. Hoover amassed nearly 50 percent of the vote, with Franklin D. Roosevelt getting less than one-third and Norman Thomas polling the remaining 20 percent. Hoover's support was spread across the nation, with the exception of the South. The incumbent won at such universities as Maine, Chicago, Minnesota, Washington, and Wisconsin. The editor of

New York University's *Daily News* commented, "The student poll reflects the thoughts of average young voters and cannot be dismissed by politicians."

In a far-reaching but flawed study done to determine the nature of student political attitudes during the 1930s, Erland Nelson discovered that, contrary to popular opinion, the students he tested were "definitely inclined toward conservatism." The questions asked dealt with more than sixty controversial issues, including free trade, race relations, military training, and alternative economic and political systems. The results indicated that the majority of undergraduates were on the conservative side, or "supporting the *status quo*," with less than 10 percent being radical, defined as favoring "fundamental social change." While Nelson surveyed more than 3,700 students, his sample was marred because out of the eighteen colleges the students attended, fourteen were private, religious institutions located in the Middle West.

In one of the few areas where there is no debate regarding the nature of student views, all observers agree that the overwhelming majority of college students were adamantly opposed to America's participation in a future war. A poll taken in 1933 by the *Daily Herald*, the student publication at Brown University, indicated that a large majority of undergraduates in sixty-five colleges across the country were against American involvement in war. Of 21,725 students who responded, the largest number—8,415—advocated total pacifism, with more than 7,000 stating that they would fight only if the United States were attacked, while the remaining 6,000 declared they would serve in any war involving America. A similar poll taken in 1931 by the Intercollegiate Disarmament Council found that 92 percent of the 24,000 students who responded were in favor of a worldwide reduction in armaments, while 63 percent urged disarmament by the United States regardless of what other countries decided to do.

Studies and polls conducted at individual colleges reaffirmed student hatred of war. A study of more than 200 undergraduates at San Jose State College in 1934 revealed that nearly 50 percent of the students believed that war was "unjustifiable and should be abolished," while 25 percent declared that "only defensive war is justified." Paul Farnsworth tested 321 freshmen at Stanford in 1932 to determine their opinions on war, and then retested them during the next four years. His results in 1934 and 1936 indicated a "sweep toward pacifism." In a poll taken in 1935, Ohio State University students voted more than 2 to 1 that the United States "must avoid war," and a majority vowed that they would never fight for their country in any foreign war. Finally Carl T. Pihlblad found that of the 535 students he tested at the University of

Missouri, 89 percent were "strongly opposed to war." He had hoped to determine what social and educational backgrounds affected such attitudes, but he discovered that income level, religion, and past education had no significance on student opinion regarding war. His conclusion—one, I think, all researchers would agree with—was, "There seems to be a surprising unanimity of opinion."

The college student of the 1930s did not undergo any dramatic shift in his or her physical appearance and remained conservative in moral attitudes and sexual behavior. Change did, however, occur in most students' life styles and political views, change that proved to be significant because it involved students for the first time in the broader societal issues of war and peace and the protection of civil liberties.

2

THE BEGINNING YEARS, 1930-1933

While the majority of the people and leaders of America were contending with the collapsed economy of the 1930s, student political activism flourished as never before. Student protest had a long and mixed existence in the United States, and was firmly established as a means for initiating and hastening reform in higher education. The crucial difference between student activities prior to 1930 and those that came afterward was that college students had never before organized into large political groups. In the thirties, undergraduates took part in both political conflict with university authorities and coordinated nationwide efforts to alter existing conditions within the United States. The Depression, the rise of Fascism, and the increasing threat of war, brought new issues, new anxieties, and new forces to the college campus. In these years the first student movement in America came into being. As one participant commented, "This was no bunch of kids getting out of hand; this was an organized opposition ... which hit very hard, and very near home." (Meyers, p. 12.)

Traditionally, this student movement has been discounted or downgraded by most scholars, usually because of either a lack of information or personal bias. Anthony M. Orum, the author of a recent study on politics and youth in America, concluded typically that the student activities of the 1930s "remained largely those of the youth branch of adult organizations," while Clark Kerr, a former university president, surmised that during the Depression, students were only "campus auxiliaries to the off-campus dissidents—trade unionists, socialists, and communists of the Old Left." The inference of both men was that student political dissidents were not acting on their own, had little impact on the social order, and were thus of minimal significance. Because students did not affect actual political decision-making, however, has nothing to do with the nature of the activities they engaged in, nor with the number or types of students involved in the movement. All sorts of protests, demonstrations, and turmoil occurred that reached beyond the control of any adult organization, and the overwhelming majority of the participating students had no relationship with any "off-campus dissidents."

Lewis S. Feuer, who has written the most extensive and subjective account of the student movement, feels that the entire affair should be excluded from serious study because it failed to "contribute to the strengthening of American democracy and the development of clear thinking." He asserts its activities, like those of other student protests, were "warped" by patterns of "generational revolt," which "imposed irrationality on the political process." The student movement of the 1930s was bankrupt, according to Feuer, because while students should have concentrated their efforts to curb Adolf Hitler, they were instead fighting to stop war.

As the decade began, many observers lamented the inactivity and lack of interest of undergraduates. The editors of the *Outlook and Independent* remarked early in 1932 that "in the future, as in the past, America will have to struggle along and solve her problems without the aid of her college students. If political change is necessary, no student bodies will lead the voting. If revolution comes, there will be no Harvard or Columbia students on the barricades." Indeed the 1930s opened with student agitation taking standard forms and involving traditional concerns. At Harvard, undergraduates wrote letters to the *Crimson,* the student newspaper, criticizing the building of an unsightly chapel with "a mammoth tower," declaring that "the administration has long . . . disregarded undergraduate opinion." At Yale, students protested "the control of [their] destinies by wealth, however philanthropic, and above all by mere traditionalism." The big revolt during the spring semester of 1931 at the University of California, Berkeley, was the cry of dental students demanding a change in the school's secret grading system, the policy of destroying examination papers, and the "glaring disregard of the honor system on the part of the faculty."

Astute observers of the college scene, however, were able to perceive even prior to 1930 that something new was stirring on campus. During the late 1920s, several colleges encountered attempts by students to reform established decision-making processes, giving more power and representation to concerned undergraduates. At City College of New York, students voted to allow the student council to oversee the school's athletic program. At Princeton, students adopted the council form of government, replacing the senior board, more than 90 percent of the student body voting to establish "an independently powerful student council, with executive, legislative, and judicial powers." At Ohio State, undergraduates demanded the creation of a director of student affairs, arguing, "There is no such thing as student government on this campus." Writing in 1928, and speaking primarily of the lack of motivation on the part of teachers, Addison Hibbard of the University of North Carolina perceptively noted that "probably at no time since the beginning of higher education in America has the criticism of our colleges and universities on the part of student bodies everywhere been so general and so bitter as it is today." And this was only the beginning.

The student movement of the 1930s was ignited by two radical youth groups, working separately—one, Socialist; the other, Communist. In 1905 a small band of intellectuals led by Jack London, Clarence Darrow, and Upton Sinclair had formed the Intercollegiate Socialist Society, whose primary object was "to create students of Socialism, not to produce Socialism." Though the executive committee included only one undergraduate—Harry Laidler of Wesleyan—members diligently toured universities throughout the country preaching the Socialist cause. After the First World War, the society was renamed the League for Industrial Democracy, and by 1927, student membership exceeded two thousand, with some seventy-five college chapters in existence. By 1931 the league's membership had grown to more than three thousand nonstudents and more than thirty-five hundred students. So successful were its organizers that by December 1932 the student division of the league was strong enough to become largely autonomous, changing its name to the Student League for Industrial Democracy and beginning publication of its own monthly magazine.

In December 1931, Communist students in New York City formed what they hoped would be a militant student organization, the New York Student League. The following February, the group changed its name to the National Student League (NSL), and began establishing contacts with students outside the city. According to its founders, the purpose of the National Student League was to organize students throughout the country to deal with those problems that had begun to appear on college campuses, and "flare up in sudden and spasmodic protest." Despite some pretensions of being a mass student organization, the NSL was recognized by most undergraduates as being a "Communist outfit." A student at New York University explained that this was true not because of anything the National Student League did, but because "it invariably presented only the Communist point of view."

One of the first actions of the National Student League was to sponsor the sending of a student delegation to Harlan County, Kentucky, where a violent and embittered coal miners' strike was taking place. On March 23, 1932, approximately eighty students mainly from colleges in New York City, but also from such schools as Harvard, Smith, Tennessee, and Cincinnati, departed from Columbia University by bus to Harlan County. The National Student League hoped that the pilgrimage would serve as an educational experience and help to bring to an end student complacency.

Hardship and strife had long been a reality in the mining areas of Harlan, Bell, and Knox counties, Kentucky, and constant wage cuts had finally resulted in the miners calling a strike in the spring of 1931. Battles raged throughout the summer and fall, as hostility steadily increased between the operators and the miners. Student involvement in the strike actually began in the summer of 1931, when Arnold Johnson, a Union Theological Seminary student, had gone to Kentucky to investigate the miners' struggle for the American Civil Liberties Union. Johnson reported that the miners "were starving, but determined to win." Their strike had been disavowed by the United Mine Workers, and many of their leaders were being held in jail by local officials on a variety of charges. "They are political prisoners," Johnson concluded. (Chatfield, p. 187.)

Most of the students in the NSL delegation expected violence. One of the leaders remarked, "I see no reason why there shouldn't be a fight. We're not going down to provoke the sheriff, but most of us are impressed with the seriousness of the venture from a historical point of view." The sheriff, not as impressed with the historical dimensions of the journey, and faced with the prospect of having "100 or more college students" arrive in his county, threatened to "file them along with other exhibits in the Harlan jail if they don't watch their step."

After surveying the situation and attempting to interview the antagonists, the students were confronted by the Harlan County sheriff, district attorney, and an angry crowd of local citizens. They were instructed to return immediately to their buses and leave the state of Kentucky, which they did. To insure their departure, "three armed deputies rode along in the bus." After their rapid exit from Kentucky, the students traveled to Washington, D.C., to air their grievances. There a government official informed them that their petition would be turned over to the Department of Labor.

Most of the delegation reacted bitterly to what they had experienced. One student concluded, "We found the press corrupted, the county government controlled by the coal operators, and the governor evasive." Charles Schrank, a student from City College of New York, remarked that "a definite reign of terror has been inaugurated in Kentucky." He described the crowd that confronted them as "gun thugs," and remembered what the Harlan County district attorney, Walter B. Smith, had told the group upon their arrival: "You're not in the United States now; you're in Kentucky. Smith is the law here." Another delegate, Rob Hall, added, "We have taken our story to two governors, three senators, [and] the president [sic] of the United States. . . . Only in the case of one lone senator was there any show of interest in a situation which we recognize as intolerable, unconstitutional, and inhuman." (*Student Review*, May 1932, p. 9.)

Although the students were turned away from Kentucky before they were able to do much to alleviate the plight of the miners, it would seem that this initial effort on the part of the National Student League was an effective one. The event attracted nationwide attention; the reaction of the Harlan officials only increased the publicity given the event; and some college students and faculty felt a few repercussions. A few weeks after the incident, more than 150 students and teachers from several Midwestern universities met at the University of Chicago and set out on a tour of the Illinois coal belt. Faced by a response similar to the one the Harlan group received, most turned back; those who did not were arrested and put in jail. In addition, over 175 prominent educators from nearly every New York City college issued protests against the "cruel repression of striking coal miners seeking to change intolerable conditions." The list of professors protesting the occurrences in Harlan and Bell counties included such figures as Rexford Tugwell and Max Lerner. The emotional experience of the Harlan expedition, with its violent confrontations and resultant publicity, acted as a catalyst for the student movement of the thirties.

Another event that helped to spark student unrest was the suspension of Reed Harris, a student journalist, at Columbia University. The incident would serve as a model for activists for the remainder of the student movement. It involved massive demonstrations by students against a university administration, the first student strike of the decade, and centered on the issues of freedom of speech and press.

When Reed Harris became editor of the *Spectator*—Columbia's undergraduate newspaper—in the fall of 1931, there was little reason to suspect that his policies and attitudes would be any different from the traditional, conservative ones of past *Spectator* editors. However, Harris's editorials soon began to focus on a number of controversial issues. He attacked Columbia's Reserve Officers' Training Corps (ROTC) program, charged there was an excess of commercialism in the school's football program, and pleaded for unemployment insurance for the nation's workers. Finally, he reopened an old wound when he demanded an investigation of the college's food service. Harris not only said that the food in the dining halls was poorly prepared, as students had maintained previously, but declared that the management of the dining halls was receiving rebates from the food dealers.

The day after the new demands and charges were made, Harris was informed by the administration that his "registration had been cancelled." The official statement declared that "material published in the *Spectator* during the last few days" was "full of discourtesies, innuendoes and misrepresentations," which called for "strong disciplinary action." Resentment against Harris' suspension was immediate. On the Monday following the administration's action (which had occurred over the weekend), a crowd of some four thousand students met on the steps of Low Library to protest the decision and formulate plans for a campus strike.

On Wednesday, April 6, 1932, the first student strike of the period took place, with over three-fourths of Columbia's student body refusing to attend classes. The students gathered around the statue of Alma Mater, in front of Low Library, and listened while speakers denounced the administration. "On Strike" buttons were worn by the students, and numerous placards were visible. Many considered the strike to be the start of a "civil war," as firecrackers and tear-gas bombs were heard exploding. Football players heckled the protestors and threw eggs, several of which hit Alma Mater. The Reverend Elliott White, class of 1891, then reportedly climbed up the statue, and "with a clean handkerchief, carefully wiped away the stains." One of the strikers remarked that at least one good thing about the turmoil was that the "football men are going to class for the first time in their lives."

The student committee which had been formed to investigate the matter declared that determining the validity of the charges regarding the condition of the dining rooms and food was not important. What was involved, they maintained, was "the right of an editor of a newspaper . . . to make charges and demand an investigation in a matter of public interest," an issue they considered to be "an aspect of the right of free speech and free press." Within a week the administration agreed to investigate conditions in Columbia's dining halls, and two weeks later, it was announced that the major demand of the strikers had been granted—Reed Harris was reinstated. Although Harris promptly rebuked the move and "resigned" from the college, the strikers claimed a total victory, one they labeled as "magnificent."

The student strike held to protest the suspension of Reed Harris is credited by many observers for ushering in the student movement of the 1930s. Although student strikes had occurred prior to the thirties, this marked the first time that a strike had a definite political theme or character about it, and the strike remained a form of protest that activists would use throughout the decade. One writer has characterized the Columbia demonstration as "a bold and almost unprecedented move." (Lee, p. 62.)

The Harris incident also brought college students together. A delegation of City College of New York undergraduates participated in the Columbia strike, and by April 12 over forty college newspaper editors had signed a petition protesting the actions taken against Reed Harris. The editor of the Indiana *Daily Student* asserted, "This is the first time in the history of college journalism that an attempt has been made to unite editors of college papers in the interest of a free press." Many of the strikers saw the event as a harbinger of what might be accomplished if college students united. The Social Problems Club at Columbia declared that the lesson students had learned was "a valuable one," that students "should feel gratified over this victory," and that they "must now organize for new ones." A Columbia alumnus, Dr. John R. Neal, saw the strike as the "most significant event which has occurred in the college world in a decade," and concluded that the students of his alma mater "have fired a shot which will be heard around the college world."

Following on the heels of the Reed Harris event, two other celebrated cases occurred in New York City—one at Columbia University and the other at City College of New York—which involved the dismissal of two instructors by their respective administrations for what both men alleged to be their radical political beliefs, views that they had made readily known to the campus community. Each firing resulted in large demonstrations, exposure for national student organizations, and helped to make the issues of civil liberties and free speech viable ones for the blossoming student movement.

In the fall of 1932, Oakley Johnson, an English instructor at City College of New York's evening session, received notice that his services would not be needed the next academic term. The administration stated that the dismissal was the result of a decreased enrollment and the return of other teachers previously on leaves of absence. What the administration maintained was an economic decision, however, soon became a rallying point for student activists.

Johnson asserted that the action stemmed from his sponsorship of the college's Liberal Club, which was associated with the National Student League, and from his open support of the Communist party. Johnson, a college instructor for twelve years, had long been involved in political matters. He had belonged to the League for Industrial Democracy, the National Student League while at the University of Michigan, and an interracial group called the Negro-Caucasian Club. In addition, he had traveled with the student delegation to Harlan, Kentucky, and had testified before Congressional committees which were conducting hearings on various pieces of proposed legislation. On one occasion, Johnson replied to a Congressman's inquiry that he "intended to vote Communist in the coming election."

Editorials soon appeared in campus newspapers demanding Johnson's reinstatement. The *Student* called the decision "administrative autocracy," and viewed the action as "the greatest violation of free speech in CCNY's history." The president of the college, Frederick B. Robinson, defended the move, citing it as only temporary and based on economic, rather than political, considerations. Nevertheless, on October 26, several hundred students met to protest the dismissal and decided to march on the administration building. Urging students that were attending class to come out and join them, the activists entered the building and paraded through the halls. The police were summoned, and they arrested twenty students. This action resulted in more than one thousand students marching to the courthouse and staging another demonstration.

The Johnson affair, which lasted for several months as students were suspended and then reinstated, marked the first major confrontation at City College of New York—a school that would become a leader in the ensuing student movement. The incident polarized the atmosphere, as students became intolerant of the administration, and the administration remained hostile to the demands of the student radicals. Many saw the event as having far-reaching implications. One student declared that the dismissal of Johnson was "an obvious threat to the instructors and students whose political and economic beliefs the college administration considers radical and dangerous." An outside observer concluded that the situation at City College of New York involved "the entire question of the freedom of student expression in the university." (Weyl, p. 16.)

In April 1933, Donald Henderson, an instructor for five years in the Economics Department at Columbia University, was informed that his contract would not be renewed for the following academic year. The administration stated that Henderson's dismissal was based on his failure to obtain his doctorate and upon his poor teaching record. A fellow instructor remarked that "Henderson has failed consistently to apply himself seriously to his duties . . . and to maintain the standards of teaching required by the department." Although the president of the University, Nicholas Murray Butler, assured students that "no issue of academic freedom is involved," Henderson claimed that Columbia was maneuvering to ease him out "without raising the question of academic freedom," which he believed to be the central issue.

The determination of why Henderson was dismissed is complicated because, like Oakley Johnson, Donald Henderson had a persistent record of involvement in radical activities. During much of 1932 he had served as executive secretary of the National Student League, playing an active role in designing plans for the Harlan expedition. He had also participated in organizing the Reed Harris strike, and in the fall he had been arrested for disorderly conduct while waiting to speak to students at City College of New York. In December he was unofficially informed by Professor Rexford Tugwell that he would not be reappointed, and he was subsequently offered the position of a university research assistant at a salary seven hundred dollars less than the one he had been receiving, with the stipulation that "the year be spent in the Soviet Union." Henderson refused the offer.

On April 20, 1933, 150 Columbia students met to protest the firing of Henderson. Several weeks later more than 1,000 students engaged in a near riot, as activists were heckled by students supporting the administration, with both groups reportedly throwing eggs and tomatoes. The "boiling point" was reached on May 15, when 1,500 students "participated in a hectic six-hour demonstration," during which fistfights, egg throwing, and "verbal harangues" took place. The highlights of this last demonstration, as the semester ground to a close, occurred when Henderson supporters carried a "black-draped coffin" onto the library steps, inscribed with the message: "Here lies Academic Freedom."

Donald Henderson, however, was not rehired, as the end of the academic year brought a halt to Columbia's second major confrontation between student activists and the administration in little over a year's time. The editors of the *Student Review*, the journal of the National Student League, concluded:

The crime of Don Henderson . . . is that he has fought for his radical ideas. Instead of talking, Henderson acted; he carried his classroom out into the world. He roused the American students from an alarming apathy and awakened an unexpected intelligence. For this he is expelled.

Acrimony between politically radical instructors and conservative college administrations did not end with the Oakley Johnson and Donald Henderson incidents. During the thirties, most state boards of education and university trustees seemed to shift their concern away from a teacher's conduct in matters of individual morality to that of public expression. After 1930, twelve states joined Rhode Island, which in 1917 had passed legislation requiring its teachers to swear their loyalty to both state and federal constitutions. At first, high school teachers were either reprimanded or fired for their political activism, but the bans on free speech spread quickly to the colleges. In numerous cases administrations censored student newspapers and barred controversial speakers from appearing on campus (topics to be examined in later chapters), as well as dismissing radical faculty members. This sort of activity persisted as late as 1939, when Dr. Charles H. Fisher, president for sixteen years of Western Washington College of Education at Bellingham, Washington, was dismissed by the board of trustees, but was given no explanation as to the cause of his firing. Fisher, however, had long been under attack by local conservatives, including the editor of the city's newspaper, for not being sufficiently patriotic, and for limiting the number of "Christian leaders" who could speak at the college. Fisher maintained that the newly elected governor, as well as the board of trustees, had acted under pressure from members of the American Legion and Ku Klux Klan.

To reiterate, the central, overwhelming reality of American life in the thirties was, without doubt, the Great Depression. Wherever one went, one saw evidence of the economic misery that saturated the decade. And yet, while the Depression was the primary consideration for most Americans, the vast majority of students were not themselves engaged with the economic issues or problems of the day. Although a nationwide activist youth movement erupted, it was not because of the Depression.

The most commonly accepted view of why there was so little student protest over the collapse of the economy is that young people retained their faith in the basic institutions and traditional values of America. Recessions and depressions had periodically come and gone since the end of the Civil War, and there was little reason to doubt that this depression, too, would soon drift away. Even if the average student no longer believed that prosperity was just around the corner, he still had a sublime faith that the corner existed and that with patience it would be reached. While few young people believed capitalism to be at the root of the country's troubles, most did not.

A more subtle explanation for this development is hinted at by Harold Laski in an article he wrote in 1931, entitled "Why Don't Your Young Men Care?" Laski, a British professor who was teaching at Yale, had visited several American colleges, and had come to the conclusion that while students were concerned with political problems and showed great interest and insight, they did not feel it was their responsibility to find solutions to these problems. Laski recalled that when the discussion reached the point of proposing possible courses of action, the student "seems to feel that this is outside the field of his concern, . . . that action is a matter for government." Evelyn Seeley, who also toured various colleges during the thirties, observed that undergraduates were no longer politically indifferent as they had been in the twenties, but like Laski, pointed out that while students were upset with the economic and political situation, they were not "interested in explaining exactly what they want."

Student activism, then, during the decade of the thirties was marked not by a concern over the nation's economic ills, but rather by a continuing agitation aimed at focusing public opinion on what appeared to students to be the world's rush toward war. Indeed, the one characteristic of the student movement that nearly all participants and scholars would agree upon is that the greatest impetus to the movement came from the peace issue, as activists attempted to ban future American participation in a war. Thus, when college students finally rebelled, it was over an intense emotional issue, and one that did not seem to require a complex solution.

The first years of the student movement witnessed a flurry of antiwar activity on the part of college students across the nation. One of the crucial aspects of this activity—one most scholars have missed—is that the various protests, demonstrations, and meetings were not staged, planned, or manipulated by any national student organization. The two largest groups—the National Student League and Student League for Industrial Democracy—became primarily involved with the war issue only in late 1933 and 1934, when the student antiwar movement became organized and official. In other words, the central element of the student movement of the thirties, the desire to keep America out of future wars, originated from the students themselves and not from student organizations.

This contention is supported by the various polls taken in 1931 (discussed in the previous chapter) which indicate a wide opposition to American military preparedness and strong support for disarmament, before any organized student movement had an opportunity to influence undergraduate opinions. Also in 1931, when a group of students at the University of California, Berkeley, formed the Social Problems Club, which was affiliated with the National Student League, its stated objectives throughout 1931 and 1932 were the achievement of academic freedom, an immediate decrease in student fees at the University of California, and the desire to "establish the American student as a political force . . . in the domestic affairs of this country." The issue of war and peace was never discussed in any publication of the organization.

Moreover, when the Student League for Industrial Democracy in its first publication in October 1932 (originally entitled *Revolt*, but changed after two editions to the less controversial *Student Outlook*) stressed what it believed should be the main concerns of students and young people in America, it urged undergraduates to mobilize sentiment on the campus against poor working conditions, to fight higher tuition fees, to start new courses on "the Economics of Depression," and to protest violations of civil rights. It was not until mid-1933 that the editors of *Student Outlook* dealt with the issue of war. In an editorial entitled "Refuse to Fight," they discussed the polls that revealed unmistakable undergraduate antiwar sentiment, and urged their readers to refuse to serve in any future wars.

The editors of *Student Outlook* noted perceptively, and perhaps reluctantly, that no activity that the Student League for Industrial Democracy had ever sponsored had caught undergraduate interest throughout the nation "so completely as the question of whether students should refuse to fight." A member of the National Student League recalled some thirty years later that while the NSL was always seeking to reveal the "deeper political significance of the issues" as they would develop in some campus protest, in reality, "college students responded to the real issues themselves." And to the vast number of student activists, the real issue was the prevention of United States participation in war.

One of the more untidy aspects of writing history is that any activity or circumstance that is supposed to have begun in a particular year, always began far earlier, and such is the case with student concern about war. In 1925, at City College of New York, a peace club was organized, beginning its stay on campus with a symposium entitled, "What Can the College Man Do About War?" Its strategy was to "research and study the problems facing those who desire lasting world peace." One of the club's main activities was to raise funds to send students abroad to secure international goodwill and friendship. For the students of the 1920s, the optimum way to promote peace was not through protests or strikes, but to develop "close fraternal feelings . . . and personal relationships with foreign students."

Beginning in 1927, and continuing throughout the 1930s, "peace caravans," led by students of the Quaker faith, toured the country during the summer months spreading the cause of peace. By 1930, one hundred and twenty-five college students had participated in the caravan program, established under the auspices of the American Friends Service Committee. Traveling in teams of two to five students, the caravans organized meetings, spoke to various youth, church, farm, and labor groups, and taught full-time classes, all in an effort to deal with the "problems involved in creating attitudes and establishing peaceful processes which will eliminate war."

The fall semester of 1931 at City College of New York encountered the beginning of a strenuous peace campaign on the part of most student groups. The *Campus* advocated the creation of a Peace Department at the school, winning the support of the students and faculty, but not the administration. A variety of student activities occurred in early 1932 to

protest Japanese presence in Manchuria. Two national college sororities—Kappa Alpha Theta and Alpha Omicron Pi—passed a resolution urging the boycott of all Japanese silk. The *Daily Maroon*, at the University of Chicago, reported a survey showing a large majority of students "would decline to fight for the protection of American interests in the Orient."

In February 1932, at the University of Southern California, a group of students declared itself "against the resort to war to decide international misunderstandings." The students asserted that their movement was different from others, because it included "the cord-wearing, football-playing type of collegian, and not the ordinary fanatic on world peace." While agreeing to defend America if attacked, they insisted they would never engage in a war outside the nation. The first university-wide open forum held at the University of California, Los Angeles, in 1932 had as its topic of discussion, "Peace and Disarmament." Students attending listened to experts on world affairs examine various aspects of the subject. A "Student Anti-War League" was formed at the University of California, Berkeley, in October 1932, consisting of ten campus organizations. Its initial activity was to hold a symposium on the causes and imminence of war.

The year's antiwar activities culminated in December when 680 delegates from colleges and universities across the nation gathered in Chicago for the first Student Congress Against War. The convention brought together a wide spectrum of groups and opinions—although those on the Left predominated—including Socialists, pacifists, Communists, labor representatives, and Christian fundamentalists. They voiced their disapproval of the League of Nations and the World Court as being unrealistic, and heard Jane Addams appeal to students everywhere actively to resist all wars and violence. The congress adopted resolutions to oppose imperialistic war, to support American recognition of the Soviet Union, and to make plans for mass demonstrations against ROTC. According to a delegate from Columbia University, however, the most important accomplishment of the congress was "the creation of a permanent organization to express student opposition to war." The *Student Outpost* at the University of California, Berkeley, concluded that an "American student movement against war was definitely set under way."

The year 1933 saw a rapidly increasing amount of antiwar activity by college students. On January 22, the Southern California Student Conference Against War convened at the University of California, Los Angeles. Over three hundred students, representing twenty-nine colleges in California, attended the two-day sessions. The highlight of the last evening session, attended by over fifteen hundred students, was to be an address by Albert Einstein, endorsing the "youth movement against war." Due to a previous engagement, however, Einstein failed to appear, and the students listened instead to famed Socialist Upton Sinclair deliver a ringing attack on war. The conference closed as students passed resolutions against militarism in college, in support of the recognition of the Soviet Union, and against the suppression of academic freedom, as well as pledging to "expose the conformity of their own professors to the current wave of jingoism."

On April 14, a contingent of eight hundred Japanese sailors and cadets arrived at the University of California, Berkeley, to tour the campus. What they found was an aggregation of student activists, who while technically holding a demonstration against imperialism, met the sailors at Sather Gate and offered them antiwar handbills. Several of the men took the leaflets, which were printed in Japanese, but as soon as the commanding officer saw what was happening, he ordered the sailors to tear them up. University officials called in the police to prevent a "physical encounter" between the groups, and the confrontation soon came to an end.

During the fall semester, antiwar conferences were held at Columbia and at New York University, with over four hundred students turning out for each gathering. At New York University a resolution was adopted protesting the use of university facilities and resources "for the dissemination of war propaganda . . . and the development of war machinery." At Cornell University, a "regiment" of women students was organized to help rid the campus of compulsory ROTC. Twenty female students handed out pins bearing the slogan "Duck the Goose Step." The reason for the uprising was the refusal of the school's trustees to approve optional military training, after the faculty and students had voted overwhelmingly to change the procedure. At the University of California, Los Angeles, the local chapter of the Student Peace Committee announced that it would begin circulating a "national antiwar petition" to be sent to the President and Congress. The students explained that the basis of their concern was "the impending crisis in both Europe and the Far East" and the "rapid growth of nationalism and militarism in the world."

During the last week of 1933, the three largest national student organizations, ranging from conservative to radical in their views, held their annual meetings in Washington, D.C. The National Student League  gathered at Howard University for its third such convention, with 250 delegates from fifteen states mapping out a strategy against war, ROTC, and Fascism. Meeting at the luxurious Mayflower Hotel was the National Student Federation, a more conservative, traditional student organization, representing student councils from more than 250 colleges. Its members discussed such vital issues as "the honor system and petty thievery in the locker rooms." They rejected an invitation to participate in a demonstration against war because "it was too radical."

The third organization holding a convention was the Student League for Industrial Democracy. The main topic for discussion was what students could do to facilitate an end to war. In addition, delegates from the Student League for Industrial Democracy and the National Student League, along with representatives from the Intercollegiate Disarmament Council, the YMCA, the YWCA, and the National Council of Student Christian Associations, established a National Conference on Students and Politics to create a framework through which young people could become permanently involved in dealing with the nation's domestic and foreign problems. Their advisory board included Charles A. Beard, John Dewey, Reinhold Niebuhr, Norman Thomas, and Senator Robert Wagner. If there is a date when the student movement became official, it would probably be December 1933.

The initial focus of the antiwar student activists was to make compulsory ROTC an optional course on college campuses. The issue was first broached at City College of New York on Armistice Day 1925. The editor of the *Campus*, Felix Cohen, wrote a review of a textbook used by the school's military-science department. In addition to the critical essay, Cohen published a few choice excerpts from the manual, including such topics as the proper methods to gouge out eyes and inculcate the desire to kill. Cohen was immediately prohibited by the City College administration from any further discussion of ROTC in the *Campus;* several weeks later a vote of the student body revealed that a large majority was opposed to compulsory military training. The issue remained clouded, until the fall of 1928 when the faculty voted to remove the mandatory feature from the ROTC program. This followed the suspension of two students who had made "disrespectful remarks" about faculty members who supported ROTC. An administration official predicted that the decision to make the program optional would "take the militancy out of the rebels."

Opposition to ROTC during the twenties was not confined to City College of New York; agitation against it also occurred in such universities as Missouri, Ohio State, Boston, Colorado, Nebraska, and Washington. In 1931 the results of a poll taken at seventy colleges with over twenty-five thousand students responding, showed that students, by a 5 to 1 ratio, opposed compulsory military training, but that only 40 percent believed that ROTC should be dropped from the university curriculum.

Protests against compulsory ROTC increased significantly during the 1930s. At the University of Nebraska, in February 1931, the student council went on record as opposing required military training, by a vote of 17 to 3. A committee was formed "to go before the proper authorities and state the council's stand." After presenting a series of pro and con articles on ROTC, the editors of the New York University *Daily News,* a conservative student newspaper, concluded that they could see little reason to keep the course compulsory. "Many intelligent observers" they declared, "fail to comprehend why prancing around in a uniform with a gun on one's shoulder is the best possible way to make a student polite, alert, healthful, clean or anything else except bored and annoyed."

In March 1932, the faculty at the University of Wisconsin voted to abolish the obligatory requirement of military training. The undergraduate newspaper, the *Daily Cardinal,* declared that the decision marked "the end of a fight which has been carried on for more than four years, and is indeed a landmark in university history." Prior to the first plebiscite ever held at the University of California, Los Angeles, on the question of military training, the *Daily Bruin* asserted that it was opposed to both optional and compulsory military training: The "spirit of R.O.T.C. is not one of inquiry. It is neither impartial nor interested in investigations of the various methods of defense against war. It is simply in the business of selling one doctrine, peace by preparations for war." In the election, UCLA students voted against the continuance of compulsory training by a ratio of more than 2 to 1.

Not all college students and administrators, however, were opposed to ROTC. At the University of California, Berkeley, the editors of the *Daily Californian* criticized those students who were attacking the ROTC program on campus. They maintained that the military department was as "opposed to war as the most outspoken pacifist." The purpose of ROTC, they declared, was not to turn out men educated in war, but to produce men "with a knowledge that would enable them to understand the workings of an industrial concern." At Ohio State University, eight undergraduates were suspended for refusing to participate in a military-training drill. The president of Ohio State, George Rightmire, observed that "the ever-increasing hordes of conscientious objectors responsible for the ROTC fracas" were most probably "just bluffing their way out of a required course." Perhaps not wanting to anger the president, the academic senate decided not to publish the results of a poll which showed that the majority of the Ohio State faculty opposed compulsory military training, declaring it might result in "some unfair publicity for the university."

The most explosive demonstration that occurred over the issue of ROTC took place at City College of New York in May 1933. The administration agreed to allow the school's military-science department to hold its annual review in the main stadium of the college. Upon learning of this decision, student radicals decided to stage a protest rally outside the stadium while the ROTC review was taking place. On May 26, the *Student* urged all undergraduates to participate in the counter-demonstration on "Jingo Day," arguing that only by attending such events can "the peace movements in the colleges succeed in wiping out the warmongers and their jingoistic propaganda."

On May 29, seven hundred demonstrators turned out to circle the stadium with placards and banners, and to try to force their way inside. At this point, the most dramatic and debated incident occurred. President Robinson, escorting guests to the review, rounded the street corner and was about to enter the stadium. What happened next is uncertain,—whether the protestors attacked the CCNY president, as he claimed—or whether Robinson raised his umbrella and "fell on the mob like a dervish," as student witnesses insisted. President Robinson later told authorities that "in order to protect my guests, it was necessary to clear the way, which I did with my umbrella." Regardless of what actually happened, the affair produced the most sensational bit of publicity that had come out of the student movement—the president of a major college disputing physically with his students.

Following the altercation, the administration suspended or expelled more than twenty students and revoked the charters of the student clubs that had participated in the protest. On June 7, over eight hundred students staged an "umbrella parade" against the administration's actions. The central attraction was an enlarged replica of the "weapon" that Robinson had employed in his tiff with the demonstrators. Between the Oakley Johnson affair and the "Jingo Day" demonstrations, twenty-nine City College of New York students had been expelled and twenty-seven others suspended. In addition, a number of student publications were either closed down or strictly censored. The actions of President Robinson had, however, gained a great deal of sympathy and support for the activists. As the *New Republic* concluded, "any college president who descends to fisticuffs with his undergraduates has destroyed his usefulness as the preceptor of youth."

Although activists were encouraged by scattered victories, their struggle against ROTC was not only a long, arduous one, but it never seriously threatened military training in the nation's colleges. By 1932, nine schools had made ROTC an elective, but only a handful had dropped it completely, and the War Department had replaced them with others. By 1938, only North Dakota had prohibited compulsory drill in state-supported institutions. As one scholar has observed, antiwar activists "faced a military establishment with large resources of finances, influence, and congressional good will." (Chatfield, p. 156.)

Protestors were also thwarted by the United States Supreme Court in their efforts to make military training optional. In 1933, the court refused to overturn an adverse judgment involving a conscientious objector at the University of Maryland, and in a case involving two students at the University of California, Los Angeles, ruled that constitutional guarantees of religious liberty did not permit college students to refuse military training in state universities. Previously it had maintained that exemption from military service is a privilege granted by Congress, not a right under the Constitution.

Beginning with the expedition to Harlan, Kentucky, to aid the striking coal miners, the student movement of the 1930s spread rapidly on college campuses across the nation, focusing on alleged violations of civil liberties of both students and instructors, and more profoundly, on a desire to prevent American involvement in future wars. A variety of antiwar activities—conferences, symposiums, protests—eventually would culminate in 1934 in America's first nationally organized and politically motivated student movement, highlighted by antiwar student strikes that would involve hundreds of thousands of undergraduates.

3

ACTIVISM, PROTEST, AND CONFLICT
The Student Movement Comes of Age, 1934-1936

Although the student movement began earlier, it came of age between 1934 and 1936, and had a noteworthy impact on American society. Student activism climaxed with large-scale organized demonstrations occurring on campuses from California to New York, and with opposition to the militants coming from conservative students, college administrators, and political leaders. By 1936, most people could no longer ignore America's first nationwide and political student movement.

As 1934 opened, it appeared that the nature of student activism was unchanged; antiwar conferences continued to dominate the student scene. On February 24, 175 delegates from sixteen colleges assembled at Smith College for the Connecticut Valley Student Conference Against War. Representatives from such colleges and universities as Amherst, Dartmouth, New Hampshire, Yale, and Trinity were welcomed by the president of Smith College, who declared, "Peace cannot be achieved by an act of Congress, you must sit at these conferences." The student delegates proceeded to pledge to refuse to support their government in any war it chose to undertake, and to seek the abolition of ROTC on campus with the available funds being used instead for "education and complete academic freedom." In March, an antiwar congress was held at City College of New York, where students listened to a variety of speakers denounce war. The National Student League captured control of the conference, which had been sponsored originally by a committee representing the views of students other than Communist. The congress voted unanimously to oppose both ROTC and "any attempt by the government to propagandize preparedness."

Then, in April, the Student League for Industrial Democracy and the

National Student League launched what in the words of one participant seemed "a rather wild idea," but what turned out to be the most successful single device of the entire student movement—a "Student Strike Against War." The event took place on April 13, beginning precisely at eleven o'clock, thus commemorating the hour that Congress had declared war on Germany in 1917. It was a simple demonstration, scheduled for one hour, with students instructed to go to their assigned classes, then to get up and leave the room and join the strike.

Twenty-five thousand students participated in the strike, most of them from colleges in New York City. At City College, the scene of the largest demonstration, students "cheered speakers who denounced war, paraded for peace, and adopted resolutions . . . against war." At Vassar, five hundred women students, led by the college president, marched through the streets, chanting, "No more battleships, we want schools." The highlight of the Vassar demonstration may well have been a song written by a Vassar senior, Caroline Hoysradt, and sung by activists. The chorus went as follows:

> Baa baa bomb shell, have you any will?
> No sir, no sir, I'm just here to kill.
> Little bomb, who made thee, who gave
>   you your mission?
> A money grasping crook and a dirty
>   politician.

One of the significant moments of the strike occurred when activists everywhere affirmed their hatred of war by taking the Oxford pledge. In February 1933, the Oxford Union in Britain had voted by 275 to 133 that "this House refuses to fight for King and country in any war." The action found a sympathetic and eager audience in the United States, as undergraduate journals devoted columns to the importance of the resolution. It was not long before American student leaders translated the pledge into a refusal "to support the United States government in any war it may conduct."

While most demonstrations proceeded quietly, protestors at a few colleges met resistance from students opposed to the strike. At Harvard, members of the Michael Mullins Chowder and Marching Club, clad in towels and displaying "Down with Peace" signs, tried their best to interrupt the antiwar activities. One of the club members came dressed as a Boy Scout, and another as Adolf Hitler. Every time a speaker would denounce war or the ROTC, the Boy Scout would blow a bugle and call for a cheer for war, while his friend would urge a "Heil Hitler" and sympathetic students would respond with a Nazi salute. The confrontation ended with the two groups battling in a barrage of eggs, oranges, and grapefruit.

At John Hopkins University, ROTC members fired decayed vegetables at the strikers, and turned water hoses on the speakers, blasting them "right off the platform." At Columbia University, twenty-five hundred students who had gathered to hear antiwar speeches by Reinhold Niebuhr and a number of Columbia professors, were forced instead to listen to Eugene S. Daniell, a young Bostonian, who was known best for placing "a stench bomb in the fan room of the New York Stock Exchange" in August 1931. Daniell, who jumped on the stage and grabbed the microphone, declared that "man is not entitled to a damn thing if he will not fight for it with his fists." Strikers retaliated by tossing an omelet at Daniell, but it was reported that "keen-nosed detectives quickly confiscated a bagfull of eggs." ("Students Wage," p. 34.)

Activists also faced opposition from several college administrations. At Hunter College, in New York City, the president threatened any student who participated in the strike "with a refusal to recommend her for a teaching position." At the University of Syracuse, nearly three hundred students took part in the protest, despite the fact that the administration barred the student paper from mentioning the strike. At the University of Oklahoma, the demonstration was canceled at the last moment when the president threatened that any striker would be expelled. And at Duke University, the administration declared that the leaders of the antiwar protest were members of an "anti-Duke ring" which was "centered somewhere outside the college."

Was the strike worth the effort? According to a member of the Student League for Industrial Democracy, the decade's first antiwar strike "shattered the granite-like indifference of the American student. Its impact upon the warmongers was heard in the snarls it elicited from the yellow press." He concluded, "The American student is on the move." (Lash, *The Campus Strikes*, p. 11.)

In October 1934, two of the decade's larger and more intense confrontations between student activists and university officials took place— one at the University of California, Los Angeles; the second at the City College of New York. On October 29, in the first major protest held on the West Coast, five University of California, Los Angeles, students were suspended indefinitely by Provost Ernest C. Moore. The suspended students were John Burnside, president of the student council; three other student-council officials; and Celeste Strack, a "nationally known debater and orator." Moore asserted that the four students, who were members of the student council, had used their office "to assist the revolutionary activities of the National Student League, a Communist organization which has bedeviled the University for some months." He charged that the four students had hatched a deal with the NSL, promising to place the program of the group into operation in return for the votes of radical students. Moore concluded, "the stage was set, for turning over the student activities on this campus to the untender mercy of the National Student League."

Celeste Strack, the only nonmember of the student council, was suspended for "persistent violation of the regulations of the University, including the holding of Communist meetings on its campus." Strack, a member of the National Student League, argued that the suspensions were the result of a struggle by the student body for the "unalienable rights of free speech, free assemblage, and free political action." The *Daily Bruin* predicted that the administration's decision would initiate a wave of student unrest unequaled in the history of the school.

The day following the suspensions, more than three thousand students demonstrated in front of the administration building to protest Moore's actions. The only message the provost had for the activists was that the suspensions would continue until students "clean house of this National Student League," and help to remove it from campus. The next day, in a radio broadcast, Moore declared that UCLA was one of the "worst hotbeds" of Communism in the country, and again called upon all students to support the administration. Shortly thereafter, approximately 150 fraternity men and athletes formed a club called "U.C.L.A. Americans" to unite students "in an organized effort to further Americanism and purge U.C.L.A. of communistic activity." The group's leader, John McElheney, declared he had responded to Moore's request, and that students would now take matters "into their own hands." The club stated that it was planning to pass out four thousand small American flags to prove to the community that the majority of UCLA students opposed the National Student League and did not harbor any Communist sympathies.

Expressions of sympathy and support for "the U.C.L.A. 5" came from students throughout the state. At the University of California, Berkeley, the *Daily Californian* remarked that the Los Angeles campus must be "awfully queer" to think that five students could turn over the university to the Communists, and the *Stanford Daily* put the blame for the suspensions on California's coming state election, in which Upton Sinclair was a candidate for governor, alleging that the provost was attempting to swing popular opinion away from the noted Socialist. At Los Angeles Junior College, 675 students signed a petition demanding the reinstatement of the five suspended students and the recognition of their constitutional rights.

On November 5, despite administration disapproval, several hundred students at the University of California, Berkeley, staged a demonstration to protest the suspensions. Professors were ordered to take roll and submit a list of those students who were absent from their classes. During the protest, activists were barraged with eggs and tomatoes. After several speeches the affair broke up, with students calling for "the unconditional reinstatements of all five suspended U.C.L.A. students." The leaders denied the gathering was in any way Communist-inspired or anything more than a "demonstration for free speech."

After a week, the suspensions seemed to have been forgotten at UCLA, a demonstration planned for November 6 fizzled, and little mention was made of the incident in future editions of the *Daily Bruin*. On November 7, the president of the University of California, Robert G. Sproul, came to UCLA to mediate the disturbance. Sproul reinstated the four male undergraduates a week later, declaring he had found no evidence that they "either directly or indirectly gave approval to the work of the National Student League, . . . or traded votes for radical support." The students responded that they were glad to be back, and Moore stated that he was satisfied. The following day Sproul announced that the case of Celeste Strack was still under consideration. Strack declared that she was not surprised that her name had been excluded, and hinted she was considering court action. On December 1, she was quietly reinstated. Although the incident ended without fanfare, it nonetheless marked the largest outcry of the entire decade for greater freedom of student expression at the University of California.

During the fall semester of 1934, a contingent of Italian students, purportedly attempting to "strengthen the bonds of friendship . . . among colleges and universities the world over," arrived in America to visit various campuses. The group's appearances at Yale and Columbia engendered considerable protest against the Fascist regime of Benito Mussolini. When it was announced that the Italians would be coming to City College of New York, there was immediate criticism, as many American students saw the visit as an official sanctioning of Fascism. The student council asked that the affair be cancelled; the administration refused; and by the time the Italian students left, the student movement of the 1930s had experienced its largest anti-Fascist demonstration.

At a special assembly, designed to introduce the Italian students, President Frederick B. Robinson had his remarks interrupted by jeers from the audience, conduct that Robinson labeled as "worse than that of guttersnipes." A member of the student council then took over the microphone, and declared he had a message for "the enslaved, tricked Italian students laboring under Fascism." At this point several of the Italian students jumped on to the stage and tried to pull the speaker off the platform. They were, in turn, surrounded by CCNY students, and the auditorium became a scene of wild disorder. The activists decided to meet outside to continue their demonstration.

An investigation of the incident, conducted by members of the administration and faculty, blamed neither the activists nor outside agitators, and suggested that explusions and suspensions were not the solution. The report attributed the trouble to "forces beyond our control that spring from the general economic and social conditions of our time." The authors concluded "We can no more deter the pulsating life of the city . . . from penetrating our walls than we can prevent the blowing of the wind or the falling of the rain." The majority of the faculty, however, refused to listen to the plea for lenience, voting to expel twenty-one students and suspend sixteen others.

Reaction to the dismissals came swiftly. That same day fifteen hundred students staged a demonstration in the stadium, where speakers proclaimed that "the fight against Fascism is a fight for our very lives." Support also arrived from outside the campus, as the American Civil Liberties Union, the Teachers' Union, and the New York *Post* criticized President Robinson's handling of the protest. "Dr. Robinson has been trying to keep order by strong-arm methods for a long time," the New York *Post* stated. "If the result is a plague of riots and picketings, . . . the cause may be found in this repressive attitude, . . . Dr. Robinson's methods breed guttersnipes."

Two months later, in mid-December, faculty members met again and reinstated the suspended and expelled activists, declaring that when convinced of the validity of student requests, they were ready to "listen and act accordingly." Thus in little over two years, City College of New York experienced three major confrontations between student protestors and the administration. By the end of 1934, every student organization, including the student council, at the nation's largest municipal college— more than 35,000 enrolled students—was in the control of militants. The demonstrations at the University of California, Los Angeles, and City College of New York, both involving the issue of how much power students should have in determining university policy, were an indication that the student movement was reaching its zenith, a fact that the New York *Post* observed in late 1934 when it stated that the CCNY disturbance was merely "another example of the unrest sweeping American colleges."

By early 1935, it was becoming increasingly clear that more and more undergraduates were actively involved in the student antiwar movement. Since 1930, more than one hundred conferences and symposiums dealing with the issue had been held on college campuses. Moreover, traditional

Armistice Day ceremonies, in which ROTC members would conduct patriotic services, were turning into mass antiwar demonstrations in colleges throughout the nation. At the universities of Michigan and Minnesota in November 1934, undergraduates on their way to their annual ROTC programs were surprised to discover hundreds of students meeting on the library steps, discussing the economic causes of war. Those who attended the services listened to speakers denounce munitions makers, Fascism, and the military. Finally, membership in student organizations swelled. The Student League for Industrial Democracy could count only 156 converts between 1932 and 1934. Between October and December 1934, however, the Socialists added 381 new members, and saw the circulation of their journal, *Student Outlook*, increase by more than one thousand between January and the end of the year. The student movement was surging.

On April 12, the second Student Strike Against War took place. The number of participants had increased dramatically, with over 150,000 undergraduates leaving class to demonstrate. The scope of the strike had become nationwide, with antiwar protests occurring on over 130 campuses across the country. The largest strike meetings were once again held in New York City, where ten thousand students attended demonstrations at City College, Columbia University, and Hunter and Brooklyn colleges. More than 3,500 activists, however, participated in the first antiwar strike held at the University of California, Berkeley. So massive was the turnout, that the strike leaders decided to form a permanent organization to combat war. Strikers even had campaign-type buttons made. They were small but very professional-looking and contained the message: "Support Student Anti-War Strike, April 12."

At American University in Washington, D.C., five hundred striking students listened to an address by Congresswoman Jeannette Rankin. At Howard University, six hundred students, though denied the use of school facilities, paraded around the campus. Three thousand activists at the University of Pennsylvania cheered Socialist leader Norman Thomas who urged them to "have the guts to stay out of war." At the University of California, Los Angeles, five hundred students attended the first peace strike held there. The main speaker was UCLA's own radical, Celeste Strack, who delivered her speech from the rear portion of a Ford truck. Demonstrations also took place at small colleges where student protest had never before been known. At Phillips College in Oklahoma, two hundred students—one-half of the enrollment—staged an antiwar rally; and the entire student body of eight hundred struck at the College of the Ozarks in Arkansas.

The strike seemed to spark the interest of many students. The Cornell

Daily Sun commented, "The Cornell undergraduate appears to have finally cast aside his usual cloak of apathy toward world problems." The *Daily Princetonian* stated, "The thinking and far-sighted youths of this country will no longer be restrained but will shout their defiance of war so all may hear it." Some student leaders saw the April strike as the beginning of a massive student response against the entire social system. James Wechsler of the National Student League argued that the strikers were only the nucleus of a much larger movement. While admitting that it took the "American campus" several years to erupt, Wechsler concluded that "we can now expect to see the dynamite it contains." (*Revolt*, p. 178.)

Activists at some schools once again faced resistance from fellow students and college administrations. Officials at the University of California, Berkeley, tried to stifle the protest by having eighteen members of the strike committee arrested for distributing antiwar leaflets. The stated reason for the arrest was the enforcement of a twenty-two-year-old ordinance "to prevent stoppage of the city drains." At the University of California, Los Angeles, Provost Moore, who opposed the movement, invited Dr. M. J. Bonn, a college professor who had been expelled from Germany by the Nazis, to speak on campus on the day of the strike. Moore declared that the timing of the event was merely a coincidence, and that the address "had no connection with the proposed antiwar strike."

At San Jose State College, Dr. T. W. Macquarrie, the president of the school, announced his total opposition to the strike. While pointing out that he, too, was against war, he refused to accept "the program of a disloyal group of vicious and partly demented people." President Nicholas Murray Butler of Columbia viewed the strike as a "negative" course of action, urging dissatisfied students to vent their anger at election time. At the University of Texas, a dean concluded that "the whole thing was started by a bunch of Russians from the East Side of New York."

At Ohio State University, the official alumni newsletter was highly critical of the strike, which had attracted four hundred Buckeye students. The editors of the *Ohio State Monthly* stated that they saw little reason for the strike. They declared that for one hour speakers had ranted and raved, hurled abuse, and talked of peace, but exhibited little of it. They surmised that what the demonstrators needed was "a good swift kick in the trousers." At Columbia University, a group of 125 "patriots" organized a counterprotest, and denounced the strike, alien agitators, and Senator Huey Long, whom it described as the "Louisiana Hoptoad." One of the group's leaders concluded that the strike was merely a sign of adolescent foolishness that would melt "like a frost before the warm sun when the moment of national emergency arrives."

Many student editors expressed opposition to the antiwar strike. The editors of the *Daily Bruin* were not pleased to see the strike come to UCLA. They declared that the campus was "weary and tired to death of radicals, reds, riots, and N.S.L.ers." They surmised that the only purpose the leaders of the strike had was to gain supporters for their own political movements and not to work effectively for peace. The editors of the *Daily Illini* at the University of Illinois stated that while they considered the ideals of the strike to be sincere, to believe that students could bring about movements resulting in the abolition of war by not attending eleven o'clock classes was absurd. At Fresno State College, the *Collegian* pondered whether striking was not in itself a form of violence and a technique that could lead to the "mob spirit." Finally, the editors of the *Minnesota Daily* concluded, "All of us are against war, but war cannot be crushed by emotionalism and strikes which disrupt the temper of education."

Most student activists were no doubt aware that the strike was simplifying a complicated issue, and that their actions alone would not prevent war. But, if nothing else, perhaps they hoped to convince those responsible for determining American foreign policy that war should no longer be considered a viable diplomatic alternative. Also, when striking against war, no students ever declared themselves in favor of Fascism or Communism, or opposed to internationalism or an ordered pluralistic society. Activists merely went on record as being against any American involvement in a future war.

Moreover, many students explored possible ways to insure peace in addition to the one-hour strike. For some, the answer lay in the development of friendly relations between nations. Activists at the University of California, Los Angeles, suggested that instead of the government spending seven million dollars for one battleship, seven thousand students could be given one-thousand-dollar scholarships to reside for a year in a foreign country, to learn the language and make friends. "What need would there be for battleships then?" they concluded. The University of Oregon *Emerald* observed that the country's need for defense depended largely upon the attitudes of surrounding nations to the United States and that the best way to achieve friendly relations was for American ambassadors to "preach the desirability of peace," rather than having the military point guns ominously.

In addition to opposing the yearly antiwar strikes, students, university officials, and political leaders, who disagreed with the objectives and tactics of the activists, engaged in other efforts to disrupt the movement. Most students who opposed the movement were not organized on any state or national level, and tended to be small clans of undergraduates who got together on a random number of campuses. Much of their activity was editorial in nature, and often was humorous or satirical. Several "anti-radical" groups, however, threatened the use of force against the activists, and on a few occasions, clashes erupted between the opposing factions.

The editors of the *Archive*, a graduate-student publication at Duke University, advised that when the first signs of radicalism appeared on campus, it was imperative that the administration provide means "with which this evil may be confronted, defeated, and barred from future penetration." They regretted that campus publications were usually the favorite medium used by activists to get their views across, and urged undergraduates not to allow their minds "to become polluted with the ravings of radical advocates." In late 1934, an "anti-club" was formed at New York University. Founded by a student, Walter Newman, its rules were that any one who was anti anything would be able to join, such as being "anti girls who have to know you better." Newman's theory was that every anti had an opposite anti, and that in his club they could all get together and cancel each other out. In November 1935, conservative students at the University of California, Berkeley, published a pamphlet entitled *Paunch*, which satirically criticized the activities of radical students at the school. They referred to the *Student Outpost*, the National Student League journal, as the *Outhouse*, sponsored an essay on the theme "Castor Oil and Communism," and dedicated the following poem to their adversaries:

> On a radical dome a great growth
>   of hair we see,
> Which looks like mother nature is
>   on a spree.
> And she is say I, I'll put you
>   wiser,
> Nature thrives on fertilizer.

In April 1935, a student group known as the Public Policy Association was formed to fight radicalism at the University of Chicago. The idea was promoted by fraternity men who had grown weary of the charge that their alma mater was "one of the ten most radical hotbeds in the United States." At its first meeting, speakers defended the Constitution, outlined the virtues of Americanism, and assailed Socialism, Fascism, and "Sovietism."

During the summer of 1934 at the University of California, Berkeley, The *Daily Californian*, traditionally a moderate student newspaper, fell into the hands of an arch-conservative editorial staff. The new editors urged that something be done to quell "the Communist menace," and stated that if a person were not a loyal American, he had no right to avail himself of First Amendment guarantees. They concluded that they favored the immediate formation of student vigilante groups to "*BLOT OUT STUDENT COMMUNISTS*," and forecast that such groups would be hailed by the university community. Shortly thereafter, a number of students on campus decided to band together to combat radical activity. Calling themselves the "Sentries of American Youth," they declared that they stood for the defense of the university from "all insidious influence," and concluded that they resented "the rape of true American idealism by unholy radical elements."

On September 21, 1933, two students at the University of California, Berkeley, who were selling the *Student Outpost* were tear-gassed by three young men. As other undergraduates swarmed on the scene, the attackers got into a car and sped off. The victims promised they would swear out warrants for the arrest of their assailants, but there is no indication that the guilty were ever apprehended. On May 16, 1935, a fight erupted at City College of New York when a group of ROTC men and football players attempted to take over a meeting of the Young Communist League. Several of the uninvited guests were allowed to speak, but after addressing the meeting, they and their followers seized and dismantled the platform. They then forced the club's leader to stop speaking, and the fight began.

A similar incident occurred at the University of Wisconsin that same week when a Student League for Industrial Democracy meeting was disrupted by a group of athletes. After heckling the main speaker, the athletes grabbed him and another student and threw them both into the campus lake. A small riot broke out, with members of the National Student League, who were also holding a meeting on campus that night, coming to the rescue of their fellow activists. The police were called in, and the situation soon simmered down. The college administration was successful in getting all sides in the dispute to agree to attend a university convocation. More than twelve hundred students listened to deans, chaplains, and student leaders discuss the concept of free speech.

For the most part, college administrators disapproved of the increased student activism on their campuses, and reacted in a number of ways in trying to stifle such behavior. Much of their opposition was directed at antiwar strikes and the presence of radical student organizations. The chief recipient for the wrath of many administrators however, were the editors of undergraduate newspapers, who tended to lean to the left in their political views, and were always visible targets for any angry college president.

In addition to the flare-ups that have already been mentioned, when administrations sought to repress activism, three students at the University of Pittsburgh were arrested in June 1932 at the request of the college administration, and were held in jail for nearly six hours as a result of trying to stage an antiwar demonstration. Their protest had been prompted by the fact that General Douglas MacArthur had been invited to speak at the university. Some three hundred undergraduates subsequently signed a petition to oppose MacArthur's appearance, and later decided to hold an antiwar protest, but they were denied permission. A Pittsburgh County judge, however, rebuked the college officials, declaring that the three activists had been guilty of "no more than a trivial and insignificant infraction of university rules."

In July 1935 the president of the University of Michigan, Alexander Ruthven, notified four undergraduates that they would not be readmitted in the fall, because they were "troublemakers." The four students had been involved in various antiwar and anti-ROTC demonstrations; all four were Jewish and came from other states than Michigan. Ruthven concluded that he deplored the "ill-mannered outbursts of [today's] undergraduates."

Ernest H. Wilkens, the president of Oberlin College, is a good example of an administrator who publicly supported the student movement, but who opposed much of what the activists were doing. In late 1935 Wilkens addressed the Oberlin student body and urged it not to sign the Oxford pledge. While agreeing that all wars are horrible, he argued that some wars should be supported, especially those that are "due to an invasion of the United States by a foreign government." He feared that the signing of the pledge would convince the government that colleges were "hotbeds of sedition," and that any future activity emanating from a university would thus be suspect. Wilkens asked the students instead to encourage the government to take effective steps toward peace.

Not all college officials opposed the student movement. In his opening address of the 1935 academic year, Dr. Harold Dodds, president of Princeton University, declared that the "business of education is not to destroy the aspirations or repress the restlessness of youth." He emphasized that if a student were devoid of rebel tendencies, his life after college would be unproductive and sterile. A week prior to the April 1935 antiwar strike, Christian Gauss, the dean of the college, praised student activists for challenging the accepted view that war was "inherent in the unchangeable nature of civilization." He lauded students for believing war could be eradicated from society. He concluded that the undergraduate of the thirties might be criticized for being overly optimistic, but suggested it would be "folly to accuse him of softness or lack of patriotism."

The student movement significantly changed the position of college newspaper editors. In the twenties, most editors—like most students—

were mainly concerned with football and fraternity life. At the University of California, Berkeley, the editor of the *Daily Californian* devoted most of his columns in 1928 and 1929 to discussions of the football season and the problems of campus parking. By 1937, however, as one student pointed out, a college editor had not proved his mettle until he had engaged in "a fracas with the university president, and one of the regents, the student administration, and . . . a business leader." Moroever, undergraduate editors were delving into the political and economic conditions of their campuses, communities, and country. One reason for this development was that while activists were a minority on most campuses, they comprised the editorial staffs of a disproportionate number of college newspapers. As a result, many editors were repressed by administrators who opposed the student movement, and their papers were either censored or suspended.

During the academic year 1931-1932, eight editors of student newspapers were either dismissed from college or lost their jobs, the most heralded being Reed Harris of Columbia. Twelve other editors left their posts under some degree of administration duress, but not one editor was removed at the request of any student body.

At Duke University, the administration supervised the election of student editors to all campus publications, and its criteria in selecting them were the citizenship records of each student, which reportedly were carefully filed away in the dean's office. Throughout the 1930s, officials at City College of New York sought the right to censor student publications. In October 1932, Dean Justin Moore of the downtown branch of the college suspended the *Ticker*, the undergraduate paper. His reason: "No criticism of the administration will be countenanced." In November 1933, eleven members, including the editor, of the *Main Events*, the evening session's paper, announced their resignations, stating that the administration had demanded all material be submitted for approval prior to publication.

Following the antiwar strike of April 1934, Joseph Jacobucci, the editor of the *Branding Iron*, the student paper at the University of Wyoming, was suspended for the remainder of the year. Observers believed that the action was caused by his adamant stand against ROTC and his support for the campus chapter of the Student League for Industrial Democracy, which sponsored the strike. Students of journalism at Louisiana State University boycotted classes on November 28, 1934, as a protest against the censorship of the campus newspaper and the suspension of twenty-six of their fellow students by university authorities. The students sent a petition to the president of the university demanding freedom of the campus press and the reinstatement of the newspaper staff. Presumably, the administration censored the paper on the direction of Senator Huey Long, because the editor had criticized Long for trying to get a particular football player appointed to the school's state senate without holding an election. Long, however, denied "ever censoring anything published at Louisiana State University." ("Strike of Students," p. 766.)

The most liberal editor that the *Daily Californian* ever had was Bill Murrish, who took over control of the paper in the fall of 1937. He began his tenure by devoting articles to such subjects as the amount of racial discrimination present at the University of California and the recruitment policies of fraternities, and by writing front-page editorials condemning compulsory ROTC and challenging the qualifications of the members of the Board of Regents. In December he was asked to vacate his post as editor by the paper's executive committee, and he agreed. Although correct in their assumption that activists constituted only a small percentage of the total college enrollment, too many university presidents overreacted to the threat that these "radical editors" posed, and were much too eager to dispel the popular notion that "their" school had been transformed into either a "hotbed of radicalism" or a "nursery for communism."

In addition to conservative students and college administrators, politicians also attempted to curb the growing activism on America's campuses. By the end of 1935, twenty-two states had adopted loyalty oaths for high school and college teachers. George Ryan, president of the New York City Board of Education, declared that the oaths would be used to exclude all who wished to teach "un-American or subversive doctrines." The historian Howard K. Beale, in his exhaustive account of the restraints placed upon teachers, concluded that the year 1935 witnessed the greatest number of cases of dismissal and repression of college instructors since 1919. In June 1935, Congress passed and President Franklin D. Roosevelt signed an education appropriation bill which included a provision that no salary would be paid to "any person teaching or advocating communism."

The stormiest battle over loyalty oaths occurred in New York City in early 1935 when students from various New York colleges organized to oppose the Nunan-Devaney loyalty-oath bill. The bill, then before the state assembly, required college students attending public institutions to sign an oath of allegiance to the New York State and federal constitutions. On March 7, fifteen hundred students, representing ten colleges in the state and five national organizations, flocked to Albany to lobby against the bill. Among the students who spoke was Edna Albers of Sarah Lawrence College, who remarked that while the bill was "directed at Reds and radicals," it would also deny "the right of criticism from the moderate element that we represent." Another student declared that the bill would only serve to "intensify radicalism."

On March 14, the state assembly's Committee on Public Education defeated the bill by a vote of 8 to 5, and the issue waned in New York. Moreover, by 1936 there appeared to be a slackening nationwide of the loyalty-oath craze, as seven state legislatures removed such bills from their statutes. Also, in May 1936 a Gallup poll revealed that more than 60 percent of the American people agreed that college teachers should be allowed to express their views "on all subjects, including politics and religion."

In two states, legislators created special committees in 1935 to investigate radicalism in their state universities. Following the April antiwar strike and a "red scare" campaign drummed up by the *Wisconsin News*—a William Randolph Hearst-owned newspaper published in Milwaukee—the Wisconsin state senate voted to establish a committee to probe "communism, atheism, and other perversionism" at the University of Wisconsin. Although the state's assembly refused to cooperate, the senate proceeded with its investigation, and several allegedly "subversive" professors and administrators were called to testify. In Chicago, Charles Walgreen, the owner of a drugstore chain, was successful in convincing the Illinois state senate to investigate the University of Chicago. Walgreen contended that his niece had been indoctrinated with Communist propaganda and exposed to ideas of free love while she was a student at the university. The hearings lasted only a week as the professors under attack were able to establish their innocence without much difficulty. The committee's report named only one professor, Robert Morss Lovett, as "unpatriotic," and for the most part praised the university.

After viewing the results of a poll which showed that a majority of the state's college students were either pacifists or would refuse to serve in a war involving the United States unless America were invaded, the Pennsylvania state senate voted in early 1933 to revoke the scholarships of those students who indicated they would not bear arms in defense of their country, and to grant the aid to "more deserving" students. In New York City, Charles E. Russell, chief justice of the city court, while ruling on a requested change of name for a City College student took the opportunity to denounce the school. His thoughts probably represented the views of many Americans of a student body that accepted a "free education" with one hand, and apparently sought to overthrow the school's administration and the federal government with the other. Judge Russell declared, "This institution, supported by overburdened taxpayers, is largely inculcating into its students the doctrines of Communism, so that the orderly and decent element in society are [sic] in fact educating a bunch of young Communists and Socialists" (New York *Herald Tribune*, May 24, 1933).

In one of the larger single demonstrations to occur at a university during this period, more than three thousand students marched against the school's administration at Washington State College to protest the rules and policies regarding student behavior and student power at the school. At precisely 11:15 on the morning of May 5, 1936, a "two-minute bell" sounded, announcing the beginning of the protest march. The activists were joined by a seventy-five-piece volunteer band and a sound truck which carried the principal speakers. Many of the students carried signs which read "My Mom is for it" and "Pop says it's O.K.," in response to the request made by the president of the college, E. O. Holland, that students consult their parents before striking.

The main demand of the activists was for greater student control. "What we want," they declared, "is a voice—a representation in the administration." The students maintained that the rules and practices of the college were not reflective of a "progressive spirit." They sought to alter the attitude of the administration toward such matters as academic freedom, social rules and regulations, and freedom of the press. The protest, however, was not a militant one. The organization formed to lead the demonstration—the Students' Liberty Association—was composed of members of fraternities, sororities, and the student council. Moreover, the specific items the activists sought to have changed were scarcely radical ones. For example, they wanted to extend the lockout time in the dormitories to eleven o'clock on week nights and one o'clock on weekends, to secure an end to compulsory attendance at classes, and to reach an agreement with the administration to publish all college rules that were applicable to students.

Nevertheless, the protesting students declared that if all their demands were not met by the faculty and administrative committee, they would conduct a campuswide strike that would close down the college. The committee, which met immediately, agreed to accept those demands. The student leaders had refused a plea that the administration be given time to investigate their demands, and instead had told the officials that a "simple yes or no" to each point would suffice. Before the decision was announced, the protestors had blocked the entrances to all campus buildings. However, the planned strike was called off once the committee's decision was made known. Although the demonstrators' specific requests today seem conservative, their basic demand for greater control over student affairs and the statement that what they sought most was a change in the attitude of the administration regarding the role of students on campus, had a distinctly radical implication, especially for the period of the thirties, even though the activists themselves may not have realized this.

On April 22, 1936, the third and largest student antiwar strike took place. Activists claimed that a record number of 500,000 students all across the country participated, although a more accurate figure is probably 350,000. On the eve of the strike, a student journal declared that the leaders of America "seem to be paralyzed in the face of the terrific war catastrophe that confronts us all. For us the strike has become one measure with a chance of success. We are looked to for leadership. We must not hesitate. Strike Against War!"

At New York University, twenty-five hundred students protested against both war and the "chauvinistic practices and yellow journalism" of William Randolph Hearst. For the first time, the majority of students in many black colleges participated in the strike, with large turnouts at Hampton Institute, Morehouse College, Virginia Union, and Howard University. At Wayne University, the Oxford pledge was taken by more than one thousand strikers, despite the condemnation of the proceedings by the college administration and the Detroit Board of Education. In the South, thousands of students demonstrated at Tulane University, Vanderbilt, and the universities of Texas and North Carolina.

After having agreed to sanction the demonstration at the University of California, Berkeley, President Sproul withdrew his support, and refused to permit the featured speaker, Norman Thomas, to appear on campus. As a result, more than five thousand students met outside Sather Gate in the largest single demonstration of the nationwide strike. They listened quietly as several speakers, including Norman Thomas, told them, "young men and women have the power to make or break war." Thomas also chided them for being so quiet, stating that "there must be color and life and drama in peace action," and adding that the cause of peace was not served by gathering peacefully. Sensing the importance of the event, the editors of the *Campus*, at City College of New York, declared "Two years ago the strike was primarily an educational gesture, . . . today it has matured to the point of power." They continued, "this is no altruistic crusade, . . . it is a fight for our lives."

The strike was enlivened on many campuses by the activities of members of the Veterans of Future Wars, an intercollegiate organization whose first chapter had been formed at Princeton in early 1936. The club had purportedly been established so that young men could collect their war bonuses in advance. Their motto was, "Hand outstretched, palm up, expectant." Membership spread rapidly throughout the land. During the strike, some twelve hundred "veterans" at the University of Washington took part in the funeral services "of the unknown soldier of tomorrow," with students dressed as Hitler, Mussolini, and J. P. Morgan serving as pallbearers. At Columbia, two hundred members of the "William Randolph

Hearst Post of the Veterans of Future Wars" marched in a strike parade, led by a student using a crutch for a baton.

Several weeks prior to the strike, more than 150 students at the University of California, Los Angeles, became members of the "Emily Post of the Veterans of Future Wars." They divided themselves into "brigades," which included an aviation corps, a tank corps, and a mud-throwing corps, the latter to be used for service in "future national elections." Two days later, the "Ladies Auxiliary of the Emily Post" was formed to enable future mothers and wives to visit battlegrounds and view "the undug graves of husbands and sons who will be victims in the as yet undeclared war."

A myriad of demonstrations, protests, and strikes between 1934 and 1936 enabled a once-fledgling student movement, small scale and centered in New York City, to expand into a nationwide movement with participants located on colleges and universities throughout the United States. Perhaps more than anything else the annual student Strike Against War was responsible for this development, as the editors of the *Campus* noted in 1936 when they declared that the strike "provides persistent and compelling evidence that the liberal, progressive mood on the campus is not confined to a mere handful of students."

4

THE ACTIVISTS AND THEIR LEADERS
Analyzing the Issues

Because the annual antiwar strikes attracted nationwide attention and stimulated thousands of young people to become involved in the student movement, issues tied closely to the success of the strikes require careful analysis. First, Why were hundreds of thousands of students so concerned with preventing American involvement in a future war? For many people, the bitter memory of the First World War was the primary motivation in their desire to keep the United States out of another war. Their thoughts were expressed by the authors of an article in the late thirties entitled "Keep Our Country Out of This War." These writers stated, "If the United States had not entered the last World War, the injustice of the Versailles Treaty would never have been perpetuated, and the threat of war would not be upon us." Americans traditionally had followed a policy of nonentanglement in the affairs of Europe. When they abandoned this concept, the result was disastrous. Hitler and Mussolini, it seems, were the result of America's attempt "to make the world safe for democracy."

Hugh MacLennan, the Canadian writer who was a student at Princeton during the period, recalled what it was like to be a young man during the thirties. "The First World War haunted us. . . . We were all children of the First War, and its real horrors were just being revealed when we came of age." He concluded that many young people believed "that the immutable laws of history" would make another world war inevitable. Lawrence Wittner, a leading authority on the American peace movement, states that pacifism never took a firm hold in the United States until after the First World War, "when a wave of disillusionment with the conflict swept across the country." In January 1937, a Gallup poll revealed that 70 percent of those asked believed it was a "mistake" for the United States to have entered the First World War.

To most students of the 1930s, the First World War apparently seemed to be both purposeless and anonymous. As scholars struggled to provide an adequate explanation for American involvement, many students turned to the works of playwrights and novelists for an understanding of the war. The romantic treatment of battle was redrawn early in bitter line by such authors as Erich Remarque in *All Quiet on the Western Front*, E. E. Cummings in *The Enormous Room*, and Ernest Hemingway in *A Farewell to Arms*. In addition, a number of nonfiction works had appeared discussing the atrocities of the war and the new American methods of propaganda—as, for example, Philip Gibbs's *Now It Can Be Told*, and Harold Lasswell's *Propaganda Technique During the World War*.

Perhaps equally as important in shaping student attitudes were the new historical interpretations of the origin and nature of American intervention. Beginning in the 1920s, such authors as Harry Elmer Barnes, C. Hartley Grattan, Walter Millis, and Charles C. Tansill questioned the wisdom and even the honesty of the actions and pronouncements of President Woodrow Wilson's administration that led up to the declaration of war. Those who read these books were told that the American people had been duped into war by profiteers. These suspicions were increased by three exposés that appeared in 1934: Helmuth C. Englebrecht's *Merchants of Death*, George Seldes's *Iron, Blood and Profits*, and a *Fortune* magazine article entitled "Arms and Men." Typical of these accounts, George Seldes concluded that "no reason for war remains except sudden profits for the fifty men who run the munitions racket."

Following these publications, the Nye Committee was established in the United States Senate to probe the extent to which bankers and munition makers had actually influenced Woodrow Wilson's decisions. The testimony, taken by the committee between the spring of 1934 and February 1936, revealed that these interests had indeed reaped huge profits. Thus the disgust that many students and older people felt about America's entrance into the First World War and the fear they had of any future military involvement was in part caused by the findings of Congress and by the works of leading revisionist historians. One of the reasons, then, why so many undergraduates were so concerned about war was because many public officials and scholars were also concerned.

Another reason why students were apprehensive about war was because it seemed as if political developments abroad were rapidly moving the world closer to another conflict. In 1935, Japan invaded Manchuria, whereupon China boycotted Japanese goods, and Japan retaliated the following year by landing troops in Shanghai. In 1933, students saw the xenophobic, aggressive-sounding Hitler rise to power in Germany; in 1935-36 the world watched Benito Mussolini's determination to establish an Italian Fascist empire by overrunning Ethiopia; and in 1936, Nazi Germany reoccupied and remilitarized the Rhineland. James Wechsler, who was then editor of the Columbia *Spectator*, observed that "the danger of war is advancing relentlessly upon us. It requires no lengthy analysis of the world scene to demonstrate the deadly parallels between 1914 and 1934."

On the eve of the April 1935 antiwar strike, the *Literary Digest* noted that the strike would come "at a time when all the pillows of Europe are haunted by the nightmare of another war." The editors of the *Daily Princetonian* declared that over 100,000 students throughout America "will hold strikes and meetings in solemn protest against the black pall of war that today enshrouds the world." They also pointed out that the United States Senate had allocated a near record $400 million dollars to the War Department, and ended calling on all the liberal forces on college campuses "to assemble in protest against war, . . . what with the atmosphere so threatening like that of 1914." James Wechsler observed that if the American undergraduate of April 1935 was a changed or revitalized human being, it was because "the world had changed from its post-war to its pre-war attire."

Finally, self-interest no doubt played a large part in the actions of some antiwar activists. The Wisconsin *Daily Cardinal* declared that it was only logical for students to voice their opposition to war: "To whom could the question of peace be of more vital interest than to the generation whose death warrant is signed should the world plunge into another war?" Joseph Lash, then a member of the Student League for Industrial Democracy and a leading figure in the youth movement throughout the decade, has since remarked that one of the main reasons students were so concerned about the issue of war was that they were "of the generation that would have to fight a war and were therefore more open to the mood of disenchantment with war that seized the country in the 1930s" (Joseph P. Lash to author, Feb. 25, 1974).

A significant characteristic of the student movement was that little connection existed between the members of the radical student organizations and the massive number of students who participated in the antiwar strikes and in the various other activities of the movement. The membership of the National Student League and the Student League for Industrial Democracy was never more than a few thousand, and while the leaders of these groups worked hard on planning the antiwar strikes and had succeeded in projecting the movement onto the national scene, the students who responded to the calls of protest against either the possibility of war or the suspension of a fellow student reflected neither the organizational ability of the student groups nor the acceptance of their radical philosophies.

As discussed earlier, students of the thirties were more serious-minded, socially aware, and politically liberal than their predecessors, and they were concerned about America becoming involved in another war before student organizations could make the peace issue a top priority. In addition, most activists never possessed a radical ideology. A recent study suggests that there was also a lack of ideological commitment by other Americans. Warren L. Susman, in an engaging article on the thirties, argues that contrary to historical belief, while the decade witnessed a swing to the left by many people, this new political stance was in no way tied to the acceptance of an ideology. His thesis is that the "culture" of the period was actually one of innocence rather than ideology.

Harold Seidman, who organized the first intercollegiate antiwar campaign in 1933, while he was managing editor of the *Daily Herald* at Brown University, argued two years later that activists still were motivated by traditional values. He maintained that their advocacy of pacifism was really a plea for democracy and fair play, and was more of a reaction to contemporary events than a systematic outlook. "The American student fears revolution more than he does war," he contended.

Prior to the April 1936 antiwar strike at the University of California, Los Angeles, *Daily Bruin* editors asserted that despite the fact that the strike was being planned by the campus chapter of the National Student League, nonradical students should not stay away; since the only "real solution" was for them "to come and take over this important way of fighting war," they "must not allow the Reds to have a monopoly on peace." Following the demonstration, the editors observed that the two thousand students who participated in the protest represented "every faith from Methodist to Marxist, but they all believed in peace."

Although they noted that there existed a great stir and departure from traditional points of view on the college campus, the editors of the *New Republic* declared that the student movement could not be described as either bold or radical. They pointed out that the student who joined an antiwar strike was also a devoted reader of the *Saturday Evening Post*, and that the movement lacked "a powerful vision of the new life." A member of a student organization perhaps analyzed the situation as well as anyone when he observed that the student movement was "filled by young men and women whose precise views on politics, religion, and sex . . . vary enormously, but who are alike in their quest for a free and just and peaceful world." (*Student Advocate*, December 1937, p. 3.)

Unlike the 1960s, most young people who were devoted Socialists or Communists in the 1930s did not seriously consider enrolling in college, believing that "true" radicals went "into the fields" to organize the masses. Al Richmond, who became a member and leader of the American

Communist party in 1928, states that when he graduated from high school in 1931, he "did not even consider the possibility of going on to college." While some of his fellow Communists matriculated at City College of New York, Richmond remembers that the rejection of higher education was "prevalent" in the ranks. Going to work in an industry and helping to organize the workers "was the thing to do." One of the significant results, it would seem, of this decision by many radicals to avoid going to college was that the student movement of the 1930s lost much of its militant potential.

Although the majority of activists neither belonged to a national student organization nor adhered to any radical political philosophy, those who joined the National Student League, the Student League for Industrial Democracy, and later the American Student Union were the leaders and promoters of most of the activities of the student movement, and thereby played a vital role in its success. Consequently, it is important to analyze these students and to examine why they became Socialists and Communists and joined militant national youth organizations.

The members of the national student organizations were more concerned with the political and economic problems and policies of the nation than were most undergraduates. They looked with disdain upon the liberal politicians in Washington, D.C., who refused to admit that their economic formulas were not lifting America out of the Depression and who failed to comprehend that the cause of the country's misery was capitalism. While most student leaders believed that the economic system was at the core of all the problems the nation presently faced, they understood—at least, after 1933—that most students did not agree with them, and that a successful movement would have to be structured around the issue of keeping the United States out of war. While student organizations tried at various times to broaden the scope of their activities beyond the issue of war, they seldom succeeded—once again demonstrating that the peace movement of the thirties was one of individuals rather than organizations.

James Wechsler, entered Columbia University as a freshman in 1931, knowing only that he wanted to be "some sort of journalist." At that time, he remembers, his heroes were H. L. Mencken and Heywood Broun. At Columbia, Wechsler brooded over the domination of student affairs by the faculty, and when he became editor of the *Spectator* in 1934, he initiated a front-page attack on the "faculty's greediness for power."

Writing in the early 1950s, Wechsler recalls that when he entered Columbia, he harbored dreams that life would continue unchanged, and like other future youthful Communists and Socialists, he did not plunge into radical literature or herald the beginnings of a new age. He states that he came to college "with only the haziest kind of political background." By 1934, however, Wechsler had decided to become a Communist, and he joined the National Student League to demonstrate formally his commitment. He remembers that it was not so much what the Communists were saying that motivated him; rather, it was "what other men failed to say." At a time when the frustration and emptiness of the Depression were evident on all sides, Wechsler recalls, "the Marxists came breathing certitude and salvation."

Initially, two years earlier, Wechsler had contemplated the virtues of Socialism and interviewed Norman Thomas, who was then campaigning for the presidency of the United States. He recollects falling "politically in love" with Thomas, and having the feeling that the famed Socialist was the "most impressive man" he had ever met. Wechsler later wrote to his brother that he was definitely a Socialist, and explained that his friends were not long-haired radicals, but merely people who wanted to get more out of life than "dances, women, and football." He subsequently became a Communist because he believed that the world was in "dreadful shape" and that America's economic and political institutions had to be changed drastically if a permanent solution and tranquility were going to be found. When pressured earlier by radical friends as to why he had not officially joined the Communist party, Wechsler remembers that the only reason he could conjure up was that his family might disapprove.

By 1936, Wechsler had developed serious doubts regarding his affiliation with Communism. Along with other radical student leaders, he had met Earl Browder, the leading figure in the American Communist party, to discuss the student situation. He was quite upset and confused by Browder's suggestion that the national student organizations should stress the ideas of collective security and anti-Fascism, while supposedly remaining firm to their original antiwar position. After visiting the Soviet Union in 1937, Wechsler broke with the Communists. While in Russia, he recalls, he experienced a "sense of imprisonment everywhere." He concluded that the Soviet Union was "a gray, monolithic civilization" and that his room was "probably wired." Following the outbreak of the Second World War, Wechsler became a liberal Democrat, a stance he has since consistently maintained. (*The Age*, pp. 17-45.)

In many ways James Wechsler is typical of those students who became radicals in the early 1930s and then grew disillusioned with that choice toward the end of the decade. For the most part, such undergraduates did not become radicals because they had studied the works of Karl Marx and Nikolai Lenin and became intellectually convinced that Communism or Socialism provided the best form of government. For many young people, students as well as nonstudents—what actually persuaded them to accept Communism was the state of American society; it seemed to be adrift with a minimal chance of recovery, and with little being done by the nation's leaders to remedy the situation. Wechsler states, for example, that he became tired of applauding the fact that the nation's unemployment rate had dropped from 25 to 22 percent. Warren Susman has suggested that one reason the Communist party was so successful in the 1930s was its ability to use "the obvious social and psychological needs of the period." People, with nowhere else to go, joined the party because they possessed ideals espoused by Communists, even though they had a sparse knowledge of Marxist ideology. In addition, the Young Communist League, the youth branch of the Communist party, provided students with camps to attend, lectures to hear, and discussion groups in which to participate.

Consequently, since so many students' conversion to radicalism lacked an intellectual mooring, it is not difficult to understand how, for example, a single journey to the Soviet Union might easily dislodge their conviction. Wechsler, moreover, was not the only well-known radical who shifted political directions during the late 1930s and early 1940s. John Strachey, who had been deported from America during the thirties because of his leftist activities and speeches on college campuses, and who became Great Britain's Minister of War in the late 1940s, confessed that the reason he became a "near Communist" during the thirties was due to the sense of personal inferiority he felt as a youth while attending Eton.

In 1938, J. B. Mathews, the first chairman of the Communist-dominated American League against War and Fascism, whom the *Daily Worker* called "a leading revolutionary socialist," became the research director for the House Committee on Un-American Activities. Subsequently, in the early 1950s, he enlisted as a staff member for Senator Joseph McCarthy, and carefully assembled the names of those who had been "treasonable" enough to have joined him in 1934 opposing war and fascism. Joseph Lash, who rejected Socialism for liberalism toward the end of the decade, remarked that most of his friends and associates of the thirties had either lapsed into political disenchantment by the 1960s or become energetically opposed to Communism.

A final reason why the student political activists of the thirties became extreme leftists is that the "Russian experiment" was still a new and intriguing development. Jane Addams, before her death in 1935, expressed the view of many when she concluded that what was occurring in the Soviet Union was "the greatest laboratory experiment in social science of all time." Unlike the United States, the Soviet Union appeared to be going from one economic success to another, and it seemed to be a land "where all ethnic peoples lived in harmony." In addition, a nation that was immersed in creating a new economic and political system would also be one less likely to seek interruption by becoming involved in war. At a time when many people believed that capitalism was responsible for the horrors of both the First World War and the worst depression in American history, it was only natural that students should be curious about the Soviet experiment. In the final analysis, it was the Soviet Union, not Communism, that fascinated most student radicals.

In 1933 a Socialist writer observed that most of the students who joined the Student League for Industrial Democracy did not do so because they believed in Socialism or even understood it, but because they wanted to make a commitment to radicalism. Alfred Kazin, who was an undergraduate at City College of New York in the early 1930s, explains in his revealing and candid book *Starting Out in the Thirties* what it meant for a teen-ager in 1934 to become a Socialist. He writes that he conceived of Socialism much as a Christian might conceive of the Second Coming—as a wholly supernatural event but one that had little immediate relevance to his life.

Like most young militant leftists, Kazin also had sparse knowledge of radical political literature. He recalls that he was "remarkedly detached from [Socialism] intellectually," that he spent his college days "reading Blake and Lawrence and Whitman," and that he thought of this new doctrine "simply as a moral idea, an invocation of history in all its religious sweep." Kazin felt a moral compulsion to be a Socialist because sixteen million people were unemployed and a million others were on strike. His Socialism, however, did not require a personal commitment; as Kazin explains, "I was a Socialist as so many Americans were Christians; I had always lived in a Socialist atmosphere."

5

THE INSTITUTIONAL SIDE

In addition to the protests and confrontations, another important facet of the student movement was the relationship of the federal government with the students and with the struggles of the various national student organizations. This institutional or official phase, usually overemphasized by scholars, is important in understanding the overall scope and impact that the student movement had. Prior to 1937, the only significant role the federal government had with students was a financial one. Neither the President nor Mrs. Roosevelt became involved with the student activists until the latter years of the decade. On the other hand, while most government officials ignored the growing movement, several people in the Roosevelt administration did not.

Addressing the annual meeting of the National Student Federation in December 1933, Henry Wallace, Secretary of Agriculture, advocated the creation of a "true youth movement." He hoped the students would develop a "new, vital, adventurous approach to the potentialities of the coming age." There was something altogether too smug and complacent about the youth of America, Wallace asserted, adding that there had never been a student movement in the United States because "hitherto our youth has seen fit to disagree with their elders only on superficialities." He concluded that there was more to being a student than attending football games and college dances. John W. Studebaker, the United States Commissioner of Education, speaking before the League for Political Education in early 1936, declared that education could not stand aloof from the two fundamental problems facing the world—"the war problem and the economic problem." He hoped that America's youth would work to promote the great rights of free speech and assembly in society, and place "more emphasis on public affairs in the educational process."

The effect of the Depression on education had been disastrous; total school expenditures declined for the first time in the twentieth century. At the elementary and secondary school level, some two hundred thousand teachers were unemployed by 1933. In many metropolitan areas the average high school class contained more than sixty young people. The Depression prevented colleges and universities from adding to their physical plans and maintaining the size of their faculties; private donations fell off; interest from investments decreased; and tax support shriveled. Between 1930 and 1936 income from all sources to institutions of higher education dropped 35 percent. The *Liberal Arts College Bulletin* surveyed the financial condition of 230 colleges and universities, and concluded that "in most cases the situation is desperate."

A fifteen-month study by a committee of the American Association of University Professors stated that between the years 1930 and 1936, college and university faculty members "had greater security of employment than their colleagues in many related professions." The committee pointed out, however, that this sweeping generalization ignored the fact that since 1930 there had been a 10 percent reduction in college faculty, that many young professors and instructors had been dropped, that salaries had been reduced to an "alarming degree," and that, in some cases, tenured conditions were greatly disturbed. Information collected by the United States Office of Education revealed that more than 70 percent of the colleges and universities had cut the salaries of their instructors in 1933-1934 below the scale of the previous year. Several colleges had to struggle merely to keep open their doors. Appropriations for the University of North Dakota were pared in half between 1932 and 1934, and Carthage College in Illinois was not the only school that resorted to barter when it agreed to accept coal in lieu of the standard tuition.

Although the Depression forced colleges across the country to limit services, trim faculties, and cut salaries, it did not bring about a reduction in the size of most institutions' enrollments. The American Association of University Professors declared that an outstanding characteristic of the Depression had been "the maintenance of college and university enrollment," that the effect of the economic slump had been to prevent an increase in enrollment rather than producing a decrease.

By 1930, however, a remarkable change had occurred in college enrollment. Between 1890 and 1929 enrollment had jumped 613 percent while population growth in the country increased only 92 percent. In addition, the limitation of higher education to a small elite was coming to an end. The number of young people attending college had increased from 4 percent at the turn of the century to 13 percent in 1930. Raymond Walters, a statistician who analyzed enrollment figures throughout the decade, revealed that there was a 3.5 percent increase in the number of students attending college in 1930 compared to the previous year. In 1931 an increase of nearly 1 percent in enrollment was recorded.

The figures for the fall of 1932 indicated a decrease in the number of students for the first time since before the First World War, with a drop of 4.5 percent in full-time students and 7 percent in the total number of college students. Enrollment figures continued to slip in 1933, with a 5 percent decrease in full-time attendance. At the University of California, Los Angeles, four hundred fewer students registered in 1933 than in September 1932, marking the first decrease in enrollment in the school's history. But enrollment again started to climb in 1934, with a gain of 5 percent in full-time students, and more important, an increase of 14 percent in the number of newly enrolled freshmen. At Ohio State University the freshman class of 1934 was reported to be the school's largest in sixty-one years, so impressing the editors of the *Ohio State Monthly* that they predicted it was part of a nationwide "back to college movement."

Enrollment jumped by over 6 percent in 1935 and continued to increase throughout the decade. Figures for 1939, for example, indicated a 3 percent rise in full-time students compared to 1938. Larger enrollments, moreover, were recorded in all areas of the country, with New York City leading the way. Enrollments at Columbia, New York University, and City College actually increased every year throughout the decade, as the total number of students attending New York City colleges jumped by 81 percent between 1930 and 1939.

At the beginning of the decade, some university officials had declared that the Depression would not hurt enrollments, and predicted that the number of students attending college would increase. Dr. Glenn Frank, president of the University of Wisconsin, asserted that studies of enrollment indicated that periods of prosperity and depression canceled each other. He believed that the tendency was "for depression to speed up registration." At Drake University, officials declared that economic downturns invariably "drive people to school" so that they can avoid the danger of losing their jobs in future depressions. President Thomas Atkinson of Louisiana State University argued that the scarcity of employment convinced parents that it was "the college man who landed the job." The most convincing explanations, then, for the maintenance of enrollment during the heart of the Depression and the increase in college attendance in the latter years of the decade, must include the growing realization of the economic value of education, since many young people believed it was wiser to stay in school than to join the millions of unemployed, as well as the general upturn in the economy after 1934.

Another important factor, which convinced many youths that they could afford to go to college and allowed millions of others to continue there, was the financial aid made available to students by the federal government. Young people were hit especially hard by the Depression. In 1930 it was estimated that one-fourth of the nation's unemployed was under the age of twenty-five, and by 1935 the number of youths out of work had increased to more than 30 percent. Analysts concluded that "youth has suffered more unemployment than any other element of the labor force." The newly designed programs of federal assistance, then, attempted to cope with this problem.

In November 1933 the Federal Emergency Relief Administration authorized a special allotment of funds for an experimental work-relief program for college students in Minnesota. Beginning in 1934, more than one thousand students started working at various projects on campuses across the state, earning an average of fifteen dollars a month. In February, Harry Hopkins, the program's administrator, announced plans to extend the assistance to all students "who have been unable for financial reasons to continue their college work." The project called for part-time employment for one hundred thousand students, with a budget of seven million dollars. Some colleges and universities, including Howard, Yale, Williams, Wells, Bryn Mawr, and Sarah Lawrence, rejected the proposed aid. Dr. Tyler Dennett, president of Williams, proposed that colleges pare their budgets and reduce enrollments rather than submit to a government dole. Dennett argued that every student was "not worthy of federal aid."

The National Youth Administration (NYA), a division of the Works Progress Administration, was created in mid-1935 to assume authority over federal aid programs for youth. By 1940 it had provided part-time work to 2 million students and to 2.6 million other young people not in school. In addition to extending assistance to secondary and graduate schools, the National Youth Administration offered guidance, training, and placement services to participating students. The requirements for aid were minimal. University administrations selected the students, with the main federal guidelines being that the work be useful and that students not displace any regular college employee. The federal government also insisted that students must have the ability to "do good scholastic work," and be "unable to enter or remain in college without federal assistance." Three-fourths of the students who received aid were from families whose annual incomes were less than two thousand dollars.

Students in the NYA program engaged in a variety of jobs. They stacked books in libraries, worked as research assistants, mended ancient pottery, mowed the lawn, and made relief maps for history classes. They did just about everything except serve as regular classroom instructors.

Students could work thirty hours a week, with monthly earnings averaging from fifteen to twenty dollars. Aubrey Williams, executive director of the National Youth Administration, declared that for the school year 1935-1936, financial assistance would be provided for more than 110,00 students attending 1,514 colleges and universities at a cost of $1,500,000 a month. Those receiving aid accounted for 12 percent of all college students. At the University of Kansas the registrar explained that the main reason for the school's 9 percent jump in enrollment in 1936 was "the grants allocated by the NYA." Very few scholarships were available to students during the Depression, and of those offered most were for small amounts. Betty and Ernest Lindley, who studied the National Youth Administration during the thirties, concluded that "the number of scholarships that pay all the essential expenses of a college is negligible. Without assistance from [the] NYA many students would be unable to avail themselves of even scholarships."

Although the central purpose of the National Youth Administration was to aid students attending college and young people searching for jobs, it appears that a number of public officials had other thoughts in mind when the new federal agency was proposed. In late January 1935, Senator David Walsh of Massachusetts introduced a resolution asking the Secretary of Labor to prepare plans for an agency to help solve the problems of young people. Walsh declared that this was necessary because otherwise American youth might become demoralized and "thus constitute a dangerous addition to the discontented and radical-minded elements in society." Moreover, Charles Taussig, one of the original designers of the National Youth Administration, told a rotary club gathering in November 1935 that the NYA was needed in order to prevent "young people from becoming Communists." (Rawick, p. 178.) While the student movement was not a major topic of discussion in the nation's capital, several politicians nevertheless seemed aware of both its existence and its potential impact.

The student organization that most politicians seemed to favor was the National Student Federation of America, the decade's only traditional student group. It had been founded in 1925 when student representatives from 245 colleges and universities met at Princeton to discuss United States participation in the World Court. Those attending the meeting decided to form a national organization which would meet annually. The federation remained loosely structured throughout the thirties since it did not have any campus chapters and because its membership was limited to those undergraduates who served as student-council officers in their respective colleges.

At a time when other undergraduate groups were denouncing war and mapping out plans to remove ROTC from college campuses, members of the National Student Federation, gathering at their annual convention in December 1933, rejected a proposal condemning university censorship of student publications, ignored motions which advocated an American boycott of the 1936 Olympics to be held in Germany, refused to take any anti-Hitlerian position, and avoided the issue of war and the student. In addition, southern delegates sought to ban blacks from attending the convention dance.

The following year, however, the group began to move to the Left politically. Although still refusing to participate in the upcoming nationwide antiwar strike, the National Student Federation was now urging students to support the policies of the Roosevelt administration. The editors of the *National Student Mirror*—the organization's monthly publication—declared, "When he [Roosevelt] took office, the country was on the verge of despair—today there is hopeful vitality which is everywhere apparent." The editors concluded that students should study the various aspects of the New Deal "so that they will be able to support it intelligently."

The organization also proposed the establishment of a "Federal Youth Service," a new agency which was to be part of the Office of Education. Its main function would be "to ascertain the character and ramifications of youth's needs," and to suggest solutions for the problems affecting young people. Although it never became radical, the group kept its liberal stance for the remainder of the thirties, which, as will be shown, placed it in the mainstream of other student organizations by the end of the decade.

A student group that was more liberal than the National Student Federation was the American Youth Congress. The youth congress was formed during the summer of 1934 by representatives of more than one thousand student and youth groups who met in New York City. The first several meetings were dominated by a struggle between moderate and leftist factions over the leadership of the organization. After a moderate, Viola Ilma, had been appointed the group's chairman, a contingent of Socialist and Communist students, objected. Calling themselves the radical caucus, they criticized Ilma's tight control over the youth congress's affairs. The chairman determined the agenda, the rules of procedure, and censored all speeches; the radical students demanded that a chairman be elected from the floor. After much confusion, the meeting was adjourned.

At the second session, later that evening, the delegates elected a new chairman, Waldo McNutt, from the Rocky Mountain chapter of the YMCA. After the Ilma faction walked out, this new group, representing

860 student and youth organizations with memberships totaling more than 1,500,000, immediately passed a series of resolutions. The proposals called for the abolition of the Civilian Conservation Corps because it was too militaristic, the unrestricted right of workers to join trade unions of their choice, and the beginning of a nationwide antiwar movement by the country's youth.

A committee was then created to establish a permanent American Youth Congress, and the final executive board consisted of representatives from all the major student and youth groups. The Ilma delegation held its own meeting and advocated more liberal birth control and divorce laws and federal aid to education; shortly thereafter it went out of existence. A spokesman for the American Youth Congress outlined what sort of organization it intended to be. He declared, "The American Youth Congress includes every shade of political opinion from the YMCA to the Communist, all united on one great thing: to protect the mass of American youth from the menace of unemployment, war and Fascism."

The second gathering of the American Youth Congress was held in Detroit in July 1935. More than three thousand delegates attended the meeting, including representatives from the American Federation of Labor, churches, settlement houses, and farm associations. The issue most discussed was the inadequacy of the National Youth Administration in solving the problems of young people. After lengthy debate, members adopted a Declaration of Rights of American Youth. In general language, it supported peace, favored special legislation for minorities, opposed attacks upon academic freedom, and called for unemployment insurance and the abolition of child labor.

Toward the end of the year, the leaders of the youth congress presented a detailed clarification of their domestic program, calling it the American Youth Act. For the remainder of the decade, the organization's central concern was to secure the passage of the act by the United States Congress. The proposed bill was more grandiose in its provisions than the federal government's program for youth. While the National Youth Administration provided college students with part-time work at a wage of approximately fifteen dollars a month, the youth act would have granted them not less than twenty-five dollars a month, and would also have made available numerous scholarships to qualified undergraduates. In addition, while the funds for the NYA came from a general appropriation, the youth act was to be financed by a tax to be levied on the wealthy. The bill was introduced yearly in Congress from 1936 to 1940, with the exception of 1939, but it never got out of committee.

On March 9, 1936, as hundreds of young people descended on Washington, D.C., to lobby for the bill, the Senate Committee on Education and

Labor opened hearings on the youth act. In what some of the demonstrators saw as a partial victory, the budget of the National Youth Administration was increased by more than seventy million dollars in April, and the agency's executive board was broadened to include the leaders of youth organizations. By July when the American Youth Congress convened for its third annual convention, its membership included groups representing more than two million students and young people. At the convention meeting, members established a national campaign to encourage young people to support the youth act. In February 1937 the youth congress sponsored another pilgrimage to the nation's capital to rally support for the passage of the act. Speaking before the Education Committee, James Wechsler declared that "not passing the bill would be a crime against youth."

Although their efforts failed, lobbying for the act enabled American Youth Congress leaders to meet influential members of the federal government. The organization soon became the decade's official or accepted major student organization. Between 1936 and 1939, the only student group represented on the National Youth Administration's advisory committee was the American Youth Congress. Its leaders were often consulted on youth problems by the Roosevelt administration. Moreover, the congress was the only student organization that President Roosevelt personally addressed at the White House and that Mrs. Roosevelt ever supported. By 1939 it claimed the affiliation of nearly five million young people.

The two most important student groups during the first half of the decade had been the Student League for Industrial Democracy and the National Student League. Prior to December 1935, when they merged and formed the American Student Union, the two radical organizations experienced a volatile relationship. One of the initial clashes between them occurred during the summer of 1932, when approximately three hundred members of each group attended a meeting of the Student League for Industrial Democracy in New York City. To the bewilderment of nearly fifty newcomers, the student radicals attacked not the Democrats or Republicans but one another. "The hall rocked as one faction thundered out accusations at the other, stamped feet, shook fists, and sang the Internationale."

What kept these groups at loggerheads was a combination of their ideological differences and the view held by Communists that Socialists, like other non-Communists, were serving the cause of Fascism. Beginning in 1929, the Communist world moved into its so-called Third Period, having at its base the theory that worldwide capitalism had lost its stability and was soon doomed to depression and chaos. Communist strategy was to

...cial Democrats and other leftists as being "social Fascists." In ... this policy was carried out with vigor, not only by the National ... League but also by the American Communist party, which com-... ocialists to members of the Ku Klux Klan, and accused Norman Thomas—between 1929 and 1932—of every sin imaginable.

In 1932 the National Student League began its official attack on the Student League for Industrial Democracy. With regard to the war between Japan and China in Manchuria, the National Student League charged that the Socialists were seeking American intervention in the matter and declared that this would result only in further "imperialistic control" of China. It concluded that student Socialists were the best defenders of "each national bourgeoisie against the spread of revolutionary discontent." Communist students also severely criticized Socialists for their lack of positive action. In July 1932 a member of the NSL charged that while the League for Industrial Democracy had been in existence for nearly thirty years, "it is still *preparing* its members and audiences for action." He could not understand how Socialists continued to "prate about education" after they had been confronted with the "militant and clear-cut program" of the National Student League.

At the National Conference on Students and Politics, meeting in Washington, D.C. during the Christmas week of 1933, representatives of the Student League for Industrial Democracy declined to go along with the National Student League in endorsing the Communist-led American League Against War and Fascism. What was really involved was the Socialists' persistent refusal to allow the incipient student movement to be identified with Communism. While the Student League for Industrial Democracy had agreed with the National Student League to oppose both war and Fascism, request federal aid for education, and strike out against racial discrimination, it would not agree to support openly a Communist organization. As the editors of the *Student Outlook* concluded, "We [can] see no way of separating a student movement from the wider political and economic movement in behalf of which it was organized." Thus, despite their common objectives, student Socialists refused to link their movement with the Communists.

Beginning in late 1933 and continuing throughout 1934, the National Student League altered its attitude toward the Student League for Industrial Democracy. Calls for unity now appeared regularly in the National Student League's journal, the *Student Review*. With its tardy realization that the two groups shared many views and could accomplish more by working together, the National Student League anticipated the official Communist party decision taken in late 1934, to abandon its Socialist-Fascist line, and to develop the concept of the Popular Front.

In December 1933, the executive committee of the National Student League, after initially berating the Student League for Industrial Democracy, suggested that the two organizations consider seriously the advantages of unity. Leaders remarked that the only result of a fragmented movement was "bitter and pedantic factionalism, . . . and a duplication of energies." They concluded that the advantages of solidarity were "strength in numbers and program. Unity of all students will isolate the die-hard romantics and the deliberate partisans." They stated they would be willing to convert their national convention to be held the last week of December into a single congress "of the American student movement."

Joseph Lash, editor of the *Student Outlook*, responded to this call for unity by admitting that the idea was a stimulating one, and that he was excited by the "vision of one powerful, revolutionary student movement." However, he concluded, one unfavorable factor outweighed all the beneficial ones—the National Student League "has been and still is the student wing of the Communist movement in this country." He added that the NSL still seemed intent on "substituting acceptance of slogans for forward movement and activity." Toward the end of 1934, the Student League for Industrial Democracy once again stated its basic objection to amalgamation. It maintained that while many of the goals of the two groups were similar, nevertheless, the organizations represented two conflicting ideologies, and that any united student movement "would become the arena of a bitter and unscrupulous struggle between the young communists and young socialists."

Although the National Student League renewed its plea for the creation of a united student movement the following year, several instances of hostility between the Socialist and Communist student groups occurred during the early months of 1935. Behind the coalition that organized the national antiwar strike in April 1935 lurked intense competition and strife. In Chicago, Socialist students issued instructions for anti-ROTC demonstrations, and explicitly stated that the National Student League should not be listed as a sponsor of the protest. On a few campuses a peaceful coalition existed, as was the case at the University of Oregon. At the University of California, Berkeley, and at the University of Washington, however, Socialist activists refused to cooperate with the dominant National Student League chapters. At New York University the chairman of the school's Student League for Industrial Democracy warned that if the National Student League took control of the antiwar strike, it would result in an "increased feeling of disgust on the part of the average member of the student body and just another demonstration by the Communist Party." In order to prevent this, he urged all New York University student organizations to take an active role in the planning and leadership of the strike.

In December 1935 the two groups put aside their differences and merged to form one student organization, the American Student Union. Negotiations between the groups had begun in late June. In September a meeting was held of the executive committees of each organization. There was compromise on both sides. The Student League for Industrial Democracy agreed to accept a new name for the organization (it had argued previously that the group should be called the Student League for Industrial Democracy), and the National Student League accepted the demand of the Socialists that the American Student Union could not affiliate itself with any other group without the approval of three-fourths of the members of the organization's executive council, which quashed the hope of Communist students that the American Student Union might link up with the American League Against War and Fascism.

The two student groups had originally planned to hold their convention at Ohio State University. The American Legion and several other organizations, however, exerted pressure on university authorities to ban the meeting because it represented "a revolutionary movement with Communist tendencies." The official reason given by the president of Ohio State University, Dr. George Rightmire, as to why he refused permission to the American Student Union to meet on the campus was that he was "trying to save coal during the vacation period." Consequently, the 427 delegates from 113 colleges and universities held their sessions at the YMCA in Columbus, Ohio.

The initial platform of the American Student Union called for additional financial aid to students beyond what was being granted by the National Youth Administration, full academic freedom, and the "democratization of the campus." It urged administrators to revitalize college curricula and to provide "social purpose" in education. The major items were opposition to "militarism," a demand that ROTC be made optional for college students, and an endorsement of the Oxford pledge. At the convention, a national executive committee was selected, consisting of thirty members—eleven former members of the Student League for Industrial Democracy, nine former members of the National Student League, and ten unaffiliated liberals. George Edwards, who was from Southern Methodist University and a Socialist, was chosen as the national chairman.

Joseph Lash, who was selected as national secretary, maintained that the American Student Union should not be viewed as merely a coalition of Socialist and Communist students, but as the "establishment of a new type of student organization—a non-political organization which bases itself on the struggle for the immediate needs of the American student population." It seemed that most undergraduates who had been part of an activist organization hoped that the American Student Union would successfully broaden the movement and cultivate the interests of many uncommitted students. They did not, however, want to make too many concessions merely for the sake of acceptability. The editors of the *Campus*, at City College of New York, for example, declared that "militance must not be sacrificed on the altar of a broad student movement." They nevertheless anticipated that the new organization would "transcend factionalism and serve the interests of all students."

At New York University, the editors of the *Bulletin*, who had supported neither the National Student League nor the Student League for Industrial Democracy, applauded their union, declaring that no effective stand against war and Fascism could be made unless the bickering stopped and the two groups united. At the University of California, Berkeley, the editors of the *Daily Californian* altered their previous conservative position and supported recognition of the American Student Union on campus. Previously they had opposed endorsing a university chapter of any national organization. A member of the National Student League recalled years later that he was "utterly sincere" in his belief that student unity was needed, and stated that "there were tears in my eyes" when the formation of the American Student Union was announced.

Thus, as 1936 began, it appeared that Socialist and Communist students had ceased their squabbling, and that the militancy of each of their previous organizations would continue. Typical of this view was the opinion of the editors of the *Campus* at City College of New York, who after reading the first edition of the American Student Union's journal, the *Student Advocate*, declared it was "vital, outspoken, . . . and adult as it comes to grips with real issues." They concluded that those who feared the new group would "lack the militance and vigor of its constituent groups" would find solace in the publication.

A primary goal of most student organizations was to expand the scope of the movement beyond campus problems and the issue of war, into such areas as labor relations and civil rights. Typical of this desire was the statement of National Student League leaders who argued that "pressing student issues" was merely a reflection of the "same conflicts . . . and dislocations that are causing unemployment and labor unrest." They pointed out, for example, that a successful struggle for lower tuition fees "must be taken to city hall, and ultimately to the bankers who do the thinking for the city fathers." They concluded "We are hitting at a decaying social and economic system when we take our stand against its campus manifestations."

Although student organizations never realized much success in their efforts to broaden the movement, some activists did become involved in the struggle to improve labor conditions for the nation's workers. The most publicized instance of students protesting in behalf of striking workers had been the National Student League's sponsored journey to Harlan, Kentucky, in March 1932, to aid the area's coal miners, which was described in Chapter 2. The Student League for Industrial Democracy had also been involved in this sort of activity. Beginning in 1930, the Socialist group organized labor "chautauquas," or workshops. Under this program college students spent their summers helping coal miners in West Virginia and Kentucky. They served with the miners on picket lines, ran schools for the miners' children, and organized classes for adults where the "fundamentals of Socialism were taught." Every month "woolens and linens" for the students, the miners, and their families, were "mailed out from the SLID office."

In September 1932 more than twenty students at the University of Minnesota joined members of a builder's union who were striking because of low wages. After the strike proved successful, some of the students were asked to speak at a union meeting. Also in September, students at Goucher College in Towson, Maryland joined striking workers of the Amalgamated Clothing Workers Union in Baltimore. This marked the first time that Goucher students had ever become involved in labor activities. Early in 1934 a group of students and faculty members from colleges and universities in California organized a "good-will tour" of the Imperial Valley in southern California, where trouble was brewing between farm workers and owners. One of the cars in which several students were riding was fired upon by "vigilantes" just north of Brawley. After briefly visiting their destination, the students and professors decided to return home.

During the first two weeks of February 1935, twenty-seven City College of New York undergraduates were arrested for picketing at the Vitamin Cafeteria in Manhattan, in conjunction with a strike called by the Food Workers Industrial Union. The judge dismissed the case but told the students to "spend more time at school and let the strikers take care of their affairs." In September, City College students joined striking Works Progress Administration workers. The strike was called by skilled workers demanding to be paid a union wage instead of the prevailing WPA rate. Union members staged a demonstration at City College "to enlist student support" in the fight against the Works Progress Administration. More than three hundred students attended, afterward joining workers on the picket line. In a letter from John L. Lewis, head of the coal miners' union, to the American Student Union in 1937, the labor leader declared that everyone in the Congress of Industrial Organizations involved with the goal of "establishing democracy in our mass-production industries" was aware of the "important bearing of the student movement upon our success." (*Student Advocate*, February 1937, p. 15.)

Not all the students who became involved in the labor movement took the side of the workers. In May 1934 a longshoremen's strike began in Los Angeles. Shortly thereafter, students from the University of Southern California began taking the jobs of the strikers. Reportedly the college employment office was encouraging students to work as "scabs." The same thing happened in the state of Washington when undergraduates from the University of Washington replaced striking longshoremen. One observer commented, "The first place employers went to obtain strike-breakers was the University of Washington. . . . Excellent food, brand new sheets, and first class Negro valet service convinced many [students] that the life of a longshoreman was not as bad as they had believed."

The national student organizations also attempted, with marginal success, to encourage undergraduates to become active in the fight to secure justice and equality for black Americans. The *Student Review* periodically included articles dealing with the plight of "the Negro student," describing the discrimination black students had to endure and attempting to enlist them in the student movement. In May 1935, at City College of New York, the Society for Student Liberties demanded an investigation into what it termed "blatant discrimination" against the only black member of the college track team by the Normandy Hotel in Philadelphia. The hotel's management had refused to admit the student, Welford Wilson, while agreeing to house the rest of the team. Wilson stated that he had "never experienced anything like it before." The student group also charged that the discrimination had the "tacit approval" of the coach and remaining members of the team. Beginning in late 1935, various colleges throughout the land launched a campaign to force the United States to boycott the 1936 Olympic games to be held in Berlin, Germany, because of the racial policies of Adolf Hitler. The *Campus* at City College of New York argued that "American athletes cannot participate in competition in a country whose government negates every principle of the Olympic oath."

The struggle to get student activists into the area of civil rights crystalized around the Scottsboro case. On March 25, 1931, authorities found nine Negro boys, one white youth, and two young white women riding on a freight train outside of Scottsboro, Alabama. Several white boys had informed the police that they had been attacked by a "bunch of Negroes" and thrown from the train. They declared that they wanted to "press charges against 'em." A telephone call to Scottsboro disclosed that the train had just passed through the city. After the blacks were taken into custody and placed in an open truck, the two white girls told the authorities that they had been raped by the nine blacks.

On April 19, eight of the nine "Scottsboro boys" were found guilty of rape and sentenced to die—the ninth, thirteen-year-old Roy Wright, was found guilty, but the judge was forced to declare a mistrial when seven of the jurors disregarded the prosecution's plea for life imprisonment and insisted on the death penalty. A prolonged and vigorous defense effort waged by the Communist-led International Defense Fund and the National Association for the Advancement of Colored People—which focused on the false testimony of the two women, both prostitutes—was finally successful in acquiring the release of the youths. Four of them were freed in 1937; the others were paroled from 1943 to 1950.

The quest for justice for the Scottsboro boys became a major concern not only of the Communist Party but also of the Young Communist League and the National Student League. For many young radicals, the word "Scottsboro" became synonymous with southern racism, repression, and injustice. The National Student League tried to make the nine black youths "the symbols of the oppression of an entire national minority." On a few campuses, there was scattered interest in the Scottsboro case. In May 1933, the Ohio State University *Lantern* declared, after the first set of retrials, that the case demonstrated "the futility of trying to secure a fair trial in the racially divided rural areas." It urged that the case "be moved out of Alabama."

On March 1, 1934, the Social Problems Club of Columbia University led a demonstration to protest "the legal lynching" of the convicted youths. Five hundred students participated and listened to key witnesses who pleaded that the convictions be set aside in the name of justice. In February 1935, the National Student League chapter at Ohio State University staged a rally to protest the Scottsboro verdicts. The school's administration attempted to ban the meeting because "it would be disrespectful to discuss a case still before the courts," but two hundred and fifty jammed the auditorium to learn the facts of the Scottsboro case and to listen to a condemnation of university officials. Nevertheless, although few heated editorials appeared in student newspapers and several demonstrations occurred on college campuses, the Scottsboro case never really became a popular issue for most student activists. Leaders of the National Student League and the Student League for Industrial Democracy could readily sympathize with Communist party official, William Weinstone, who concluded in 1935 that "very few members have been brought into the Party as a result of the Scottsboro campaign."

The institutional side of the student movement encompasses the role that the federal government played in relation to students and the activities and internal struggles of the various student organizations. The only significant relationship between the government and students prior to 1937 was economic, as the National Youth Administration provided part-time jobs for millions of students, enabling them to remain in school. Two of the decade's more peripheral student groups on campus were the National Student Federation and the American Youth Congress, since neither organization had individual members or campus chapters and only met once a year. The two major student groups during this time—the National Student League and the Student League for Industrial Democracy—had an acerbic relationship, caused by their differing ideologies and the view held by Communists that Socialists were aiding the success of Fascism throughout the world. They ultimately put aside their grievances and merged in December 1935 to form the American Student Union. For the moment it seemed that the bickering had stopped, and that the student movement would not lose any of its past militancy.

6

ISOLATIONISM VERSUS COLLECTIVE SECURITY

Beginning in 1936, the student movement underwent a transformation in its objectives, tactics, and spirit. The movement lost much of its militancy and appeal to students, with the majority of remaining activists no longer concerned about keeping the United States out of war. The American Student Union, dominated by Communists after 1936, urged that the United States adopt a foreign policy based on the principle of collective security. It sought primarily to encourage the Roosevelt administration to involve the nation in the fight against European Fascism. Consequently, it dropped its radical approach to campus and social issues, and supported the New Deal. By 1937 the annual antiwar strike had become a demonstration to promote American involvement in the Spanish civil war; by 1938, the conventions of the national student organizations had turned into football-type pep rallies, complete with cheer leaders and pom-poms. Noting the change in the movement early in 1937, the editors of the *Spectator* at Columbia observed, "For the first time in five years world-wide unrest found Columbia a serene home of learning, and little more."

While most Communist and liberal students were trying to alter both the appearance and substance of the movement, Socialist students continued their militant opposition to American involvement in war. The first signal of this rupture occurred during the student strike against war in April 1936. Socialists sought to maintain the tradition of past strikes, with students walking out of their classes, going to demonstrations, and taking the Oxford pledge. Communists and liberals, however, hoped to turn the strikes into peace assemblies or rallies, with the Oxford pledge being dropped, and with speeches directed at collective security replacing the strident antiwar ones. Although activists on some campuses continued to hold strikes, with students engaging in angry demonstrations, many colleges now experienced so-called peace meetings, with students gathering quietly in auditoriums to listen to speakers, with the entire affair being approved of by the school administrations.

Most Socialist members of the American Student Union were outraged at this turn of events. One of their goals for the 1936 antiwar strike had been to demand that Congress adopt genuine neutrality legislation. However, as Joseph Lash sadly reported, many protestors opposed this goal because "they wanted the nation to be in a position to participate in sanctions against an aggressor." Hal Draper, also like Lash a Socialist member of the American Student Union, charged that Communists had decided to "abandon the program and traditions of the American Student Union," in order not to antagonize liberal members. He believed that the United or Popular Front policy of the Communists would destroy the student movement. At Columbia, the response by the editors of the *Spectator* to the administration-run protest meeting was that it was "ineffective," and "dull as ditch-water," and that the direction of the event "was obviously touched with a stiff dose of Emily Post."

In December 1936, the dispute over what the American Student Union's position should be regarding America's role in the world appeared for the first time in the *Student Advocate.* In a letter to the editor, George Edwards, the national chairman of the American Student Union, who was an ardent Socialist, stated that the "impressive record" of the organization could be attributed chiefly "to the unyielding anti-war program of the Union and to its dramatic and effective summary in the Oxford pledge." He urged that the group's second convention, which was to convene later that month, "reaffirm support of our present peace program." Celeste Strack, the American Student Union's national high school secretary and a former member of the National Student League, stated in another letter to the editor that the organization's present peace program must be "implemented with a more realistic approach to the world scene." She declared that the main threat to world peace was not the United States, but "Fascist aggression," and urged that the focus of the student movement be aimed at those nations whose interest was "to plunge the world into another massacre."

Socialist strength in the American Student Union was still sufficient to get the convention to endorse the Oxford pledge and omit any reference to collective security. An anticollective security resolution, however, proposed by the Socialists, was defeated by thirty-seven votes. While Socialist, Communist, and liberal delegates disagreed over what the peace program of the American Student Union should be, there was nevertheless a strong show of unity on the basic domestic goals of the organization. For example, there was an enthusiastic endorsement of the proposed youth act, agreement on the necessity to remove from the campus compulsory ROTC, and a unanimous vote to launch a drive to secure the support of black students. By December 1937, any consensus between the Communist and Socialist members of the American Student Union had evaporated.

By 1938, the student movement had drastically altered its outlook, direction, and purpose. It was no longer militant or radical; most activists were now working closely with college administrators and government officials. The American Student Union, fearful that the belligerent advances of Adolf Hitler would go unchecked, wanted to get the United States inextricably involved in world affairs. The organization came out against the Oxford pledge, supported college dances and football games, and received the praise of President Franklin D. Roosevelt. It was difficult to find many similarities between the student movement of 1934-1935 and the one of 1937-1938.

Student protests still occurred on college campuses, but they seldom were aimed at political issues or against war. For example, at Kansas State College, students conducted a strike to demonstrate the need for a new physical science building. At Colby College in Maine undergraduates protested the closing of the "social room" in co-ed dormitories, and threatened "to sit down in it" if their demands were not met. In early 1937, student opinion at City College of New York had shifted from war and the problems of society to the fact that the student cooperative store on campus had a deficit of sixteen hundred dollars. Investigations were demanded; management was condemned; and the controversy occupied the front page of the *Campus* throughout February.

As an indication of how "New Dealish" national student organizations had become, the American Student Union in April 1937 issued a call for a nationwide student rally to support President Roosevelt's proposal to increase the number of justices on the Supreme Court. Its leaders declared that this move into the political arena was necessary because they had to convince "the student body of America" that the American Student Union was interested in "realistic action." In October, American Student Union chapters on numerous campuses held protests not to criticize the failure of Congress to pass the American youth act, but to chastise it for having cut the annual appropriation for the National Youth Administration. Student leaders asserted that the federal youth agency "affects every student in all colleges," and they planned to have undergraduates fill in questionnaires on the "need for the NYA."

The American Youth Congress, also seeking to establish an image of moderation so that it could more successfully influence the government to adopt a collective-security foreign policy, declared that its fourth annual convention in July 1937 would be modeled after Congress, with a house of representatives, a senate, and legislative committees, and with delegates discussing "matters of concern to American young people." In 1937, also, a committee, headed by William Hinckley, chairman of the American Youth Congress, and including representatives from the American Student Union, the YMCA, and the National Interfraternity Conference, was organized to assist the Works Progress Administration to secure aid for college playwrights and dramatists.

The metamorphosis of the student movement reached a quite different level of theatrics as Communist students tried to show how patriotic they had become. On April 19, 1937, the members of the Young Communist League in New York City celebrated the 162nd anniversary of Paul Revere's ride by hiring a horse and rider, dressing them in appropriate costume, and then cheering as the horse pranced down Broadway. The irony is that it seems that the Daughters of the American Revolution had forgotten that year to honor Paul Revere's day of glory.

In April 1937, also, the fourth annual antiwar strike was held, but the division and antipathy among the activists all but destroyed the event. Despite predictions by the American Student Union that "the scope of the strike will assume astonishing proportions," and that "nearly one million students" would participate, only twenty-five thousand students took part, since the broad coalition of activist groups that had helped make the strike a success in the past no longer existed.

At Columbia University, more than four thousand students had been expected to protest, but only fifteen hundred actually appeared. The *Spectator* analyzed Columbia's strike as the "smallest and most uneventful April peace demonstration in three years," a conclusion that was applicable to other protests throughout the land. The American Student Union chapter at New York University stated that twelve thousand undergraduates would turn out for the strike, but only two thousand participated. "What happened to 10,000 students?" the editors of the *Bulletin* asked. They stated that it was with "sharp disappointment that we witness this tendency on the part of students, . . . disappointment in their vigor, in their interest, and ultimately in their utter lack of perspective."

One of the more successful demonstrations occurred at the University of California, Berkeley, where activists allowed the protest to be supervised by the student council. On April 23, forty-five hundred students attended the "peace meeting" in the gymnasium. It was the first time that the annual protest had not been held as a strike outside campus. It was the first time also that the administration had granted approval of the demonstration and made no attempt to interfere with the affair's proceedings, as it had earlier. At the University of California, Los Angeles, the student council voted, on the suggestion of President Robert Sproul, to assume control of the demonstration. It decided to hold a peace assembly in the campus auditorium, stating that the "strike action" taken yearly by the national student groups was "an illogical means to an end we all desire."

Students attending these peace assemblies did not hear speakers condemn war or demand that the United States stay out of European affairs. While the official slogan of the 1934 strike had been, "Schools not Battleships, Abolition of the R.O.T.C., and Fight against Imperialist War," the theme of the 1937 strike was "Remember Spain." Activist leaders sought to convince undergraduates that they should become interested in the Spanish civil war, which had broken out in Spain in July 1936, and support the Loyalist cause.

On the eve of the strike, the American Student Union declared that the country's neutrality laws were "a sham neutrality at best and overt aid to Fascism at worst." The objective of the strike, it stated, was "to win sympathy and aid for the embattled Spanish people." At the University of Michigan, activists collected seventeen hundred pounds of clothes and eight hundred pounds of food to be sent to the Loyalists. At Stanford University students heard Chester Rowell, editor of the San Francisco *Chronicle,* advocate an internationalist foreign policy for the United States. After listening to speakers solicit aid against the forces of Spain's General Francisco Franco and urge that collective security was the way to achieve peace, the editors of the *Spectator* at Columbia, obviously longing for a return to the strikes of 1934 and 1935, described the 1937 affair as "the final prostitution of the student peace movement."

While most of the antiwar strikes evolved into quiet peace assemblies, several campuses experienced traditional strikes, and on some two protests took place, one advocating neutrality and the other supporting collective security. At the University of California, Los Angeles, the greatest number of students ever to attend an off-campus antiwar strike congregated on April 23. More than one thousand protestors chose to attend the activities rather than the administration-sponsored peace assembly held on campus where two hundred students appeared. The main speaker at the strike declared, "War never gets anyone what he really wants, . . . to have war you need fighters; to have peace you need people who refuse to fight. So I say—Refuse to Fight." Nevertheless, Socialists agreed that the antiwar strike was less successful than in previous years, pointing to "the division of ranks, and the increasing drive toward war" as the causes for its collapse.

In December at the annual American Student Union convention,

Communist and liberal members were able finally to push aside Socialist opposition to their demands. The five hundred members meeting at Vassar College dropped the Oxford pledge, adopted a strong collective-security position, and declared their goal was to work closely with the Roosevelt administration. In November, at a meeting of the organization's administrative committee, Alvaine Hollister, a Socialist, had introduced a motion that the committee go on record to endorse the Oxford pledge. The Communist members of the committee, however, labeled the idea as "isolationist," and led a successful battle to defeat the motion. Then, in December, a majority of the delegates voted to eliminate the antiwar pledge from the American Student Union's platform.

Only a year prior to this decision, the American Student Union chapter at New York University had declared that the Oxford pledge was "the rock on which the student movement was founded." Following the vote, many Socialists walked out of the convention. Alvaine Hollister declared that the action was a "betrayal of the fight against war," and vowed that Socialists would attempt to organize students outside the American Student Union.

One key element that spelled certain defeat for the militant Socialists in the American Student Union was that by 1937 a number of leaders in the organization, such as Joseph Lash, Molly Yard, and Robert Spivack, had switched their views and orientation and now advocated a policy of collective security for the United States. In December, for example, Lash stated, "The American Student Union is [now] international in outlook. There has been general agreement that our basic task . . . [is] to bring America's power for peace to play in the present world situation." He declared that the objectives of future antiwar demonstrations would be: "A campaign in support of Spanish democracy, the popularization of the boycott of Japan, . . . and the consideration of a legislative policy which we can support in Washington." (Lash, *The Campus: A Fortress*, pp. 10, 21.)

The convention voted to urge the United States to take immediate steps to restrain the actions of "aggressive" countries and to place embargoes on warlike nations. In addition, the delegates passed resolutions to boycott Japanese goods and to give aid to unions which acted to restrain trade with "aggressor nations." Moreover, they stated that the American Student Union now wanted to work closely with college administrations, and was "proud of the cordial relations" that existed on many campuses between "administrators and the A.S.U." Group leaders also hoped that the *Student Advocate* would change its format so that it would appeal to the whole student body. They sought a magazine that while still being "progressive in tone," would also possess "the attributes of the fiction weeklies and comic monthlies."

Festivities planned for the annual American Student Union gathering included an operetta, a Christmas party, and "dancing into the wee hours." The final event of the convention was a New Year's Eve ball, and according to reports, the hotel where the dance was held was "spruced up like Mrs. Astor's pet horse." Joseph Lash, in summarizing the convention's achievements, concluded that the "American Student Union has finally won recognition as the representative of the American student movement." To support his contention, Lash produced praiseworthy telegrams and letters from President Roosevelt, Aubrey Williams—the director of the National Youth Administration—and John L. Lewis. The student movement had definitely shifted its purpose and direction.

The developments and changes in the movement that began in 1936 and 1937 continued during 1938. Leaders expanded their efforts to present an image of the student movement that would be approved of by the government, the American people, and by most undergraduates. Any hint of militancy was removed. As Joseph Lash recalled, "Our pronouncements began to be phrased more calmly, our targets to be selected more realistic[al]ly." The American Youth Congress was so determined to gain administration support that it dropped the American youth act and advocated a "strengthened and expanded N.Y.A."

On March 5, 1938, the American Student Union chapter at City College of New York planned to hold "the goofiest informal dance in the history of the college," to celebrate CCNY's upcoming basketball victory over New York University. Its message to students was, "We'll have a helluva good time if you let yourself go." At Hunter College and at City College, American Student Union members created a dating-bureau service at their respective colleges during the spring term. The group's publicity director—Harold Fabor—announced that to take advantage of the service, one had to leave his or her name, phone number, the evening desired, and to specify blond, brunette, or redhead. At the University of California, Berkeley, the Young Communist League urged all students to vote for the state's Democratic candidate for governor in the November election of 1938. Leaders declared, "We Communists make no bones about it; we're 100% for American democracy." Following the election, they noted that "the majority of Californians voted where their [sic] interests lie, with the New Deal." They applauded the fact that "the Democrats . . . still hold a big majority of state offices."

In December, the American Student Union held its fourth annual convention. Approximately thirty-five hundred members, meeting at City College of New York, voted overwhelmingly to support a resolution calling for an American foreign policy that would "discourage the forces of aggression," and recommended that Congress revise the Neutrality

Act in order to give President Roosevelt a "wide discretion." The keynote address at the convention vigorously endorsed both the New Deal and President Roosevelt. Joseph Lash, who delivered the speech, urged students to "play a decisive part in the 1940 election," and to support "the objectives of the New Deal."

The convention received a warm welcome from President Roosevelt in a letter of greeting. He encouraged American Student Union members to make the college campus "a fortress of democracy," and stated that he believed student groups were working hard to improve the country's "social conditions." Most of the speakers who addressed the delegates avoided the issue of politics, and discussed such topics as the type of work undergraduates were doing in their classes, the papers they were writing, and the grades and honors they were receiving. Students listened, for example, to a college administrator who analyzed the health and housing problems on campuses, and outlined the steps that had to be taken to stimulate good health standards.

The atmosphere that engulfed much of the student movement by 1938 was evident at the final event of the American Student Union convention—a jamboree. An observer commented that the affair had "all the trappings of a big-game rally." Along with the students, there were "white-flanneled cheer leaders, a swing band, and shaggers doing the Campus Stomp." Student delegates at the jamboree sang the new American Student Union march. It went as follows: (Bliven, p. 283)

> Break thru reactions line
> Send Progress crashing thru, [sic]
> Pull together all the time
> And we'll win with the ASU, A-S-U!
> Send the roar up, roll the score up,
> On to victory
> While we rush down
> Score a touchdown
> For Democracy.

Feeling a bit defensive about the transformation of the American Student Union, Agnes Reynolds, then treasurer and secretary of the organization, attempted to justify the group's actions. She declared that "actually there is a place for gaiety in the post-Munich world," adding that students who attend football games and college dances "are very nice people and . . . would make good A.S.U. members."

The Socialist students who opposed these changes in the movement struggled throughout the latter half of the decade to return the student movement to where it had been in 1934 and 1935. Verbal battles raged between the Socialists and the leaders of the American Student Union, with the more ambitious Socialists breaking away from the organization and forming their own antiwar groups. Most accounts of the movement, for some reason, have ignored this strenuous, if unsuccessful, opposition by some Socialist students to the path taken by the American Student Union, the American Youth Congress, and most activists.

Socialist students were upset primarily with the decision by the majority of the members of the American Student Union to urge the United States to adopt a foreign policy based on collective security. They wanted the organization to continue to oppose American intervention in the affairs of other nations. A Socialist member of the group's executive committee, Jeffrey Campbell, maintained that the United States, for example, should "have no part in the Spanish struggle," arguing that wars aimed at fighting Fascism were still wars, and were "accompanied by all the characteristics which describe wars." He urged that students "clamor for a complete and mandatory neutrality as far as the American government is concerned."

Al Hamilton and Alvaine Hollister who had broken with the American Student Union, declared in 1938 that it was tragic that the organization had been transformed into "an arm of the Roosevelt administration." They saw this as an attempt by the Communists to sweep college students "into the war camp, as was done in the pre-war months in 1916-1917." They disagreed with American Student Union leaders that Fascism would cause the next war, stating that the real enemy continued to be "the clash of rival imperialist interests." Socialists believed that a foreign policy designed on the concept of collective security or internationalism, which consisted of applying diplomatic pressure on nations, declaring embargoes and selling munitions, was a policy that made war easier. They also were convinced that war was part of the problem, not the solution. As one student declared, the trouble with war was that "fighting does not bring about democracy or peace, no matter who you fight." Finally, the Socialists were suspicious of the motives of the Communists, believing that the Communists wanted to involve the United States in the Spanish civil war in order to facilitate American involvement in a future war between Nazi Germany and the Soviet Union.

Those Socialist students who opposed the policies of the American Student Union formed a number of other organizations to try to create a mood of opposition to collective security in the country. In November 1937 160 Socialists and pacifists met at Vassar College to develop a strategy to deal with the "present aimlessness of much of the student peace movement." They formed an organization, called the Youth Committee for the Oxford pledge, which was based on the idea that the key to preserving peace was to unite students behind the antiwar pledge, which they felt had become "the heart of the student movement." They urged a revitalization of the country's pacifist forces to achieve the principles of "justice, good will, and brotherhood."

On March 28, 1938, more than three thousand students at City College of New York attended a rally to protest the growth of Fascism in Spain. Speakers demanded that the United States reshape its foreign policy to fit a pattern of collective security and ship arms to the Spanish Loyalists. Simultaneously, several hundred members of the newly formed Anti-War Club on campus staged a counterdemonstration; they denounced collective security and argued that an isolationist policy was the only way a world war could be averted. Communist students did not ignore those Socialists who continued to oppose war rather than Fascism. Members of the Young Communist League at the University of California, Berkeley, for example, stated that "certain ultra-left elements" in the student community "are aiding the Fascists," when they "attempt to disrupt the growing unity of the progressive forces against reaction." They maintained that Socialists who stressed "their conflicting views" on war tended to emphasize "the disagreements within the peace movement instead of the unity."

Nearly all the Socialists who opposed the direction the movement had taken after 1935 were members of the Young People's Socialist League, the most militant student or youth group that existed during the latter years of the decade. Very often those Socialists who dropped out of the American Student Union joined the Young People's Socialist League or were members of both organizations concurrently. The Young People's Socialist League had been founded in 1907, when several groups of young Socialists organized in New York City and Chicago. It grew steadily until 1919, when it was discovered that the league's national secretary had secretly joined the Communist party. This disclosure coupled with the rift that occurred between Socialists and Communists after the First World War all but put the YPSL out of existence for the next ten years.

In 1929 some young Socialists formed a "district organization" of the Young People's Socialist League in New York City, and in 1932 the league was declared to be officially part of the Socialist party. Prior to mid-1935, the YPSL was not a radical organization. Its leaders were moderate in their views and had little confidence in radical action as a means of building the youth movement. The group, for example, had never expanded in scope, conducted recruitment drives, or attempted to discover its weak features. As one observer commented, "There was little leadership." Moreover, the league functioned largely on the belief that a Socialist youth movement should concentrate almost entirely on young workers rather than "fooling around with petty bourgeois students." (McDowell, pp. 43-50.)

At the organization's national convention in July 1935, however, a new contingent of leaders was elected: Socialists who were committed to a "left-wing leadership," and determined to be "militant as an organization." These new leaders, who were also members of the Student League for Industrial Democracy; began seriously to consider the advantages of student unity. Consequently, in December, when the amalgamation of the National Student League and the Student League for Industrial Democracy took place, the executive board of the Young People's Socialist League agreed to endorse the merger. As one member rejoiced, the YPSL could now become "a banner bearer of Revolutionary Socialism penetrating every youth and student organization with its message."

The decision to support the American Student Union was, however, not approved by every member of the Young People's Socialist League. One "yipsel" viewed the action as an "opportunistic catastrophe," and urged the league to interest itself in converting students to the "revolutionary labor movement," instead of becoming involved with "how to join liberal organizations." Another member stated that he was not opposed to unity with Communists and liberals "in action against war," but declared there could never be unity in "a theoretical program on war."

Most members of the Young People's Socialist League, however, were not critical of the American Student Union and the American Youth Congress until these organizations abandoned their antiwar positions in 1937 and advocated an American foreign policy of collective security. One "yipsel" commented that the socialists were not criticizing student Communists because they were Communists or dominated student organizations, but because they refused to support the American working class. He argued that the Communists were more interested in "keeping solid" with members of the YMCA and other liberal groups than with "the progressive trade unionists and Socialists."

In early 1938, members of the Young People's Socialist League at the University of California, Berkeley, declared that the "whole history of collective security . . . is one of complete bankruptcy." They maintained that collective security was a device used to foster "the war plans of our government," and a policy supported by the Communists to give the Soviet Union "ephemeral support against its potential Fascist aggressors." Later that year they staged a demonstration to protest any congressional attempt to repeal the arms embargo, and they withdrew their chapter's membership in the American Student Union, arguing that they found the organization to be "incompatible with opposition to imperialist war." By the end of the decade, most members of the Young People's Socialist League had decided to leave the organization in protest over the decision by the Socialist party to expel its radical members, the Trotskyites.

These dissident factions then formed a new independent group called the Socialist Workers Party.

Between 1936 and 1938 the student movement experienced a sweeping alteration of its purpose, spirit, and direction, which according to one activist "changed its face completely in mid-course." The movement lost its militancy; fewer students were involved in protest activities; and most activists were no longer interested in keeping the United States out of war. The American Student Union, controlled by Communists who were eager to have the United States adopt a foreign policy based upon collective security, dropped its radical approach to domestic issues and supported the New Deal. Although many Socialists continued throughout the decade to oppose the movement's new objectives and image, it was clear by the end of 1938 that the student movement bore little resemblance to the one that once had flourished on college campuses across the nation.

7

THE MOVEMENT ENDS, 1939-1941

The student movement in its last years experienced a continuation of both the antiwar protests and the nonideological, more traditional forms of student activism that had begun in 1937. The most important development, between 1939 and 1941, however, was the collapse of the entire movement, when the United States entered the Second World War in December 1941, thus ending the debate over what America's foreign policy should be. These years were also significant because the involvement of the President and Mrs. Roosevelt in the movement culminated during this time.

Many students still opposed any interference by the United States in the affairs of Europe. Socialists at the University of California, Berkeley, stated in September 1939 that their primary objective was "to keep America out of war." They declared that a war against Germany could never be a "good war"; it would just be a "new and brutal phase of the long-standing conflict between rival imperialisms." They concluded that "we in America must stay out. This is our first task, . . . and first duty." In the fall of 1939, a group of antiwar students at Harvard formed a "Committee for the Recognition of Classroom Generals." Members, dressed as tin soldiers and carrying armchair citations, marched into the classrooms of five "interventionist" instructors, and delivered speeches warning students about the dangers of war. It was reported that "gas-masked pickets" paraded for one hour outside the room of a particularly belligerent history professor. (Ross, p. 80.)

In 1940, Mortimer J. Adler, a professor of philosophy at the University of Chicago and an ardent interventionist, wrote an article in which he declared that the "pre-war generation" of students distrusted any cause which spoke "the language of principle." Adler maintained that most undergraduates were void of moral values and patriotism. The only ray of sunshine for Adler was the approaching war, which he hoped would reeducate students in the virtues of freedom and democracy. His views, reflecting the beliefs of others, suggest that many students in 1940 still were opposed to America's participation in war.

Most student activity, however, during these years continued to be of the fun-and-games variety. In the spring of 1939, the American Student Union at City College of New York held its first "Ask the Professor" meeting. In an atmosphere permeated with gags and puns, students grilled their mentors with such requests as "Will one of the experts sing the first line of three popular songs beginning with the word 'thanks.' " Another sign that the movement had seen more militant days occurred in March 1939 when the fad of swallowing goldfish began. A student at Franklin and Marshall College, in Lancaster, Pennsylvania, helped initiate the craze when he downed three. Before the rage leveled off, a student at Kutztown State Teachers College, also in Pennsylvania, had consumed forty-three such fish in less than an hour, and was then suspended by the school's administration for "conduct unbecoming a student in a professional course."

The New York *Herald Tribune*, pleased that demonstrations and strikes were on the wane, remarked, "If students aren't swallowing goldfish, they are up to something else . . . just as much fun at the moment. That's what keeps students from being dull." A further indication of the direction in which the movement was going occurred in late 1939 when the president of the American Student Union at City College of New York resigned in order to take an administrative position with the Civilian Conservation Corps, at a salary of eighteen hundred dollars a month.

For the leaders of national student organizations, with the changing situation in Europe forcing them periodically to reassess their position, these final years were far from easy ones. Since 1937 both the Communist-led American Student Union and American Youth Congress had favored a foreign policy based on collective security. The chapter of the American Student Union at City College of New York, for example, declared itself in support of the school's annual ROTC review to be held in May 1939. Its president stated, "We welcome the fact that the students in the R.O.T.C. share a strong concern for peace and democracy." The spring semester of 1939 brought the greatest enrollment in ROTC that City College had ever had since the course became noncompulsory. The increase of more than one thousand students represented a jump of 65 percent over the previous semester's enrollment.

After the announcement in August 1939, however, that Soviet Russia and Nazi Germany had signed a trade agreement and nonaggression pact, student organizations suddenly reversed their policies. The Nazi-Soviet pact, in addition to shattering the beliefs of many activists who had sympathized with the Soviet Union, caused the American Student Union to begin calling for strict American neutrality in the event of war in Europe. On September 3, after Poland had been invaded and Britain and France declared war on Germany, the American Student Union characterized the European situation as "imperialist," argued that both sides were equally reprehensible, charged that the New Deal had lost its meaning, and stated that the "interventionist" plotting of President Roosevelt must be stopped. The American Youth Congress, which in July 1939 had urged the repeal of all neutrality acts, emphasized in October the dangers of American involvement in the war, citing the probable curtailment of civil liberties and the erosion of the country's standard of living.

At the American Student Union's annual convention in December 1939, most of the organization's remaining non-Communist members—like the national chairman Molly Yard, Agnes Reynolds, and Joseph Lash—declared that if the delegates endorsed the invasion of Finland by the Soviet Union, which had begun on November 30, the organization would become a "narrow sect," and that the student movement would collapse if progressivism were identified "with the twists and turns of Soviet policy." The convention, however, ignored this advice, and by a vote of 322 to 49 refused to condemn the Russian attack. The editors of the *Campus*, at City College of New York, who had long supported collective security and were very leftist in their views, concluded that "the American Student Union has now formally resigned from leadership in the American student movement."

The new isolationist position of the American Student Union and of the American Youth Congress ceased in June 1941 when Germany invaded the Soviet Union. In September, officers of the American Youth Congress informed President Roosevelt that they had several ideas about how to combat the "appeasement forces" that were flourishing in the country, and declared they wanted to meet with him. The meeting, however, never took place. The final irony of the student movement is probably a mimeographed letter from the youth congress to President Roosevelt sent in May 1942, which requested his greetings to the "Second All-Soviet United Youth Meeting."

Between 1939 and 1941, however, most students, as well as the majority of Americans, lost much of their faith in isolationism as a policy. A study of twelve hundred undergraduates in the fall of 1939 revealed that more than half of the students blamed Germany for the war and favored a foreign policy structured on collective security. In 1935, 75 percent of the American people had favored holding a national referendum before

Congress could declare war; in 1939, support for this idea had dropped to 58 percent. In 1940, a poll indicated that 68 percent of those asked believed that it was more important to defeat Germany than for the United States to remain out of the war. In November 1941, the editors of the *Campus* mirrored the views of most American citizens when they declared, "We face the future with a steadfast determination and a calm sobriety . . . We must do our part in this war against totalitarianism."

This decision of whether to support an American foreign policy based on collective security or one committed to neutrality and noninvolvement was faced by most people during the 1930s, including student activists. A primary factor responsible for reshaping the objectives and tactics of the movement was the rise of European Fascism, a development that undergraduates could not control. When forced to choose between continuing to advocate the benefits of peace or emphasizing the horrors of Nazi Germany, many activists either selected the latter or became silent and dropped out of the movement.

For Socialists who had struggled throughout the decade to make the student movement a militant one opposed to all wars, the success of the Communists and liberals in transforming it into a respectable venture supporting American preparedness was an unforgivable occurrence. One Socialist student who was bitter during the thirites and remained just as angry four decades later was Hal Draper. Draper, who had been born in New York City, attended New York University and Brooklyn College, from which he graduated in 1934. He joined the Student League for Industrial Democracy in 1932, was one of the founders of the American Youth Congress in 1934, became a member of the American Student Union's first executive committee in December 1935, and was appointed as high school director of the Young People's Socialist League in April 1936. He left the American Student Union in 1937, becoming a full-time Socialist organizer and editor of the Independent Socialist League's magazine, *The New International*.

Draper has charged that by 1937 Communist students had taken the "guts" out of the student antiwar strike, and by 1938 had emasculated what was once a sincere and honest effort by young people to keep America out of another brutal European conflict. George Rawick, who has written extensively on the decade's youth movement, supports this harsh view. He maintains that the American Student Union became nothing more than a Communist party conveyor belt carrying young radical students from their "commitments" into the dreary world of "official liberalism," thus making impotent a once energetic and lively movement.

Those Socialists who held firm to their antiwar position, by no means favored the growth of Fascism. They were, however, convinced that the fight against Fascism could not be waged successfully by international war. Most militant Socialists, like Draper, believed that any war that the United States became involved in would result in a struggle to benefit and protect corporate capitalism. Their answer was to alter America's economic system, and then attempt to stifle Fascism. Irwin Ross, who wrote an article "College Students and War" in mid-1940, summarized the position of those students who bitterly opposed Fascism and yet were against American involvement in war. Ross argued that these students were not indifferent to the fate of democracy and the world. He maintained that students were aware of the moral issues and acutely conscious of the menace of Fascism, but that they differed "with their elders on methods of combating the recognized danger."

While one can sympathize with the position taken by Hal Draper and others, it seems evident that the decision of many Americans, including most Communist and liberal students, to support collective security and a strong military defense was no easy or sinister choice. By 1939 the options open to students were more difficult. While war was still viewed as repulsive, Fascism had become a possible threat to American security. It no longer seemed to most student activists that the United States would be responsible for starting the next war. In 1934 and 1935 the world had appeared to be manageable; stability and order were just beyond the horizon. In the next four years, however, things changed.

In late 1938, Hitler took over the Sudentenland of Czechoslovakia. In March 1939, he struck again, devouring the remainder of Czechoslovakia, and sneering at those who protested his activities. On September 1, he invaded Poland. In April 1940, he seized Denmark and Norway. In May, the German army swept through Belgium and raced around the Maginot Line. Nazi tanks then churned into France, cutting off British forces and driving them toward the Channel. Suddenly Hitler was toppling the balance of power in Europe and forcing war-loathing Americans to decide whether to alter their views of war or risk letting the Nazis dominate the whole of Europe.

For some people the decision to oppose Fascism rather than to continue to oppose war was not one that caused them serious inner turmoil. As historian Alan Lawson has observed, for many "the war against Fascism was grim business, but it entailed no painful shifts of allegiance or policy." Walter Millis, for example, regretted that his revisionist book, *The Road to War*, which criticized American intervention in the First World War, had made such a great impact. Attorney Charles P. Taft wrote that while he still admired the pacifists with whom he had worked in the Emergency Peace Campaign of the 1930s, "I am glad there are not too many."

For most, however, the decision to support collective security and the war was more painful. Some students believed the situation posed an almost impossible dilemma. One student argued, for example, "It'll be hell either way . . . If we go in, there will be fascism at home and American young men dead abroad. If we stay out, and Hitler wins, the necessity for huge armaments and a regimented economy may give us Fascism anyway." Many students, it seems, were more interested in peace than in supporting a foreign policy committed to collective security and possible war. In 1938, the *Daily Herald* sponsored a poll on foreign affairs at Boston University, with most of the questions concerned with the issue of whether or not students were in favor of collective security. While the results indicated that the majority of students approved of such a policy, it was reported that many wrote on their ballots that they felt the poll was designed to procure the least possible objections to collective security, adding that the only thing they desired was peace. One undergraduate declared that any policy that brought peace "is O.K. with me." (*The Campus*, April 1, 1938).

Like other students, James Wechsler did not turn to collective security because he had become a Communist. He was sincerely troubled over the realities of Nazi Germany. In late 1938, after he had bitterly renounced his association with Communism, Wechsler could not help but remark it still seemed that only "Moscow and Washington . . . were displaying any resistance to the course of appeasement that had led to Munich." For many, the consternation experienced by Rabbi Judah Magnes, the president of Hebrew University, Jerusalem, was typical. A pacifist during the First World War, Magnes renounced his former views to support preparedness, even though he believed he was transgressing God's word. He sadly concluded, "We do not know what else to do." ("A Tragic," p. 407.)

Militant Socialists also have argued that the Communist policy of a Popular Front helped destroy the antiwar emphasis of the student movement because it tricked unsuspecting liberals and anti-Fascists into supporting the Communist position. For many students, as well as nonstudents, however, the idea of a Popular or United Front appeared to be an appropriate answer to the tragic debacle in Germany. The strategy of marshaling all possible forces into one common bond opposed to the growth of Fascism did not appear at the time to be a "Kremlin manipulation," and there is evidence to suggest that the concept was initiated before the Soviets formulated it as official policy. For example, in the summer of 1934 students pushed the American Youth Congress into a stance of unity against both war and Fascism, even though it was under pressure from leaders in the American Communist party to abandon the policy. In addition, while the Popular Front theory dovetailed with the

Soviet policy of achieving a collective-security arrangement against the Nazis, one should resist the temptation of assuming that anything that corresponds to Soviet policy automatically contradicts the views and interests of other people on the Left.

Another development, which culminated between 1939 and 1941, was the involvement of President and Mrs. Roosevelt in the student movement. During his first term in office, the President had had no relationship with the movement. He had refused to send a message of greetings to the initial gathering of the American Youth Congress in July 1934, and later that year declared that there was no young people's problem; there was "only the problem of the whole people." When given a report on youth joblessness by his wife, he reportedly "shrugged it off" and handed it to an aide to read. (Lash, *Eleanor and Franklin*, p. 539) Whenever President Roosevelt discussed the youth movement, he referred only to the problem of unemployment. He had consistently refused to meet with any student leaders, but in February 1937, he agreed to see a representative of the American Youth Congress. During the discussion, Roosevelt outlined various strategies that he thought the group might use to get its youth act out of committee and on to the floor of Congress. Later that year, after a parade down Pennsylvania Avenue, in which youth congress members participated in a sit-down strike, Roosevelt consented to meet with several of the activists. He told them that they were on "the right track in seeking federal aid for the nation's hard-hit young population." In December 1938—as has already been discussed earlier in this book—the President sent a letter of greetings to the annual convention of the American Student Union, asking the organization to help transform the college campus into a "fortress of democracy."

The only formal speech given by the President to members of any national student organization occurred in February 1940, when Roosevelt addressed a "pilgrimage" of over four thousand students from the American Youth Congress on the White House lawn. It was a stern speech, in which the President defended the American loan recently given to Finland. He argued that this was in no way an attempt to involve the country in the war, characterizing such talk as "unadulterated twaddle." Drowning out a "ripple of boos and hisses," Roosevelt warned the youths not to adopt resolutions on subjects on "which you cannot possibly have complete knowledge," and he labeled the Soviet Union "a dictatorship as absolute as any other dictatorship in the world." Regarding unemployment, the President declared, "You young people must remember that the problem of the older workers . . . is just as difficult as yours." He was not convinced, he stated, that the opportunities for employment were any worse for young people now than "they were for young people . . . thirty years ago."

Columnist Walter Lippmann, applauding Roosevelt's "verbal spanking" of the students, concluded that the protestors were "shockingly ill-mannered, disrespectful, conceited, ungenerous, and spoiled." Following Roosevelt's speech, the members of the youth congress listened to John L. Lewis, head of the Congress of Industrial Organizations. Lewis, to the delight of the "spanked" students, urged the Democratic party to nominate anyone but Roosevelt for President in 1940. He mocked the President's speech, declared that his views on Finland and the Soviet Union were "like yours," and suggested that the American Youth Congress should become affiliated with the labor movement. Joseph Lash remembers that following the Lewis speech, "bedlam broke out," as the students' fondest hopes were exceeded.

Professor Robert B. Merriman, master of Eliot House at Harvard, sent Roosevelt a letter in the winter of 1940 in which he complained about the "peace-at-any-price kids" at Harvard and characterized student activists as "shrimps." In May, Roosevelt responded to Professor Merriman, agreeing that "shrimps" was a good description. Although the President believed that there were "too many" of these students, he assured Merriman that "most of them will eventually get in line if things should become worse." (Roosevelt, p. 1028.)

On June 5, President Roosevelt met with about fifty student and youth leaders, mostly from the American Youth Congress, at the White House. He answered questions for three hours, and did not resort to tongue-lashing the students as he had in Feburary. Joseph Lash, who was present, recalls that while many of the questions implied that the President had become conservative in his social outlook and no longer cared about "progressive objectives," Roosevelt patiently answered them, trying to explain "his difficulties to us as well as expound his position." One of the reasons why Roosevelt took the time to meet with the youth leaders was probably his belief that many young people in the country still favored an isolationist foreign policy. On May 16 he had delivered a speech before Congress and called for an additional fifty thousand airplanes a year and an increased production of other war material. Following the speech, many people sent letters and telegrams to the White House, most of them approving the President's requests, but Roosevelt was upset by the fact that of the twenty percent that disapproved, "most of them came from youth organizations and college students."

While President Roosevelt had a very limited relationship with the student movement, Mrs. Roosevelt experienced a far broader involvement. Between 1934 and 1940, she developed close ties with the American Youth Congress and its members. Dismissing the warnings of friends and presidential advisers to avoid the student leaders of the American Youth

Congress because they were too radical, Mrs. Roosevelt spoke before their national conventions, publicly defended them when they were attacked by Congressional committees, attended their weddings, and helped them raise money for their budgets.

In the summer of 1934, Viola Ilma, the first chairman of the American Youth Congress, invited Mrs. Roosevelt to be a sponsor of the new organization. Mrs. Roosevelt, however, unsure of the group's political leanings and purpose, declined the offer. Nevertheless, she sent a letter to the gathering in which she expressed an interest in the organization's activities, and requested a report "of the proceedings and any conclusions which you have come to." In January 1936, after radical students had captured control of the youth congress and had refused to endorse the National Youth Administration, Mrs. Roosevelt agreed to address the organization's national council. It was a stormy session. Members challenged her on the adequacy of the National Youth Administration, demanded that more money be allocated for youth problems, and seemingly "tried to outdo each other in the militancy and truculence of their questions." Undaunted, Mrs. Roosevelt openly expressed her views, won over many admirers, and concluded by inviting the group's members to the White House for further discussion.

In early 1938, Mrs. Roosevelt spoke before the opening session of the New York State Model Youth Legislature at City College of New York. This group included the most radical members of the American Youth Congress, and Mrs. Roosevelt believed she could produce a "calming effect" on them. She criticized the antiwar movement and the Oxford pledge, and outlined the harmful effects that isolationism could have on the United States. Once again, Mrs. Roosevelt was warmly received by her audience.

Perhaps the most dramatic confrontation between activists and the federal government occurred in late 1939 when several leaders from the American Youth Congress and American Student Union were called to testify before the House Committee on Un-American Activities. One of the activists immediately telephoned Mrs. Roosevelt, hoping she could prevent the confrontation. Instead she urged the students to appear and to be cooperative, and promised to meet with them the next day. President Roosevelt, after being informed by his wife of the youth leaders' forthcoming appearance, characterized the committee's methods as "sordid," and remarked that it might be possible for him to be "shipped into the hearings under a sheet." Melvyn Douglas, the actor, who was visiting the Roosevelts, observed that the President would "be welcomed as a Ku Kluxer." (Lash, *Eleanor Roosevelt*, pp. 10-11.)

Shortly after the hearings began, Mrs. Roosevelt entered the committee room. She was invited by the chairman to sit with the Congressmen at the main table, but she politely refused. The tone of the hearings changed immediately, as committee members became defensive, joked with the students, and even allowed Jack McMichael, a youth congress leader, to read a resolution which called for the abolition of the committee. When the hearings were adjourned for lunch, the students were invited by Mrs. Roosevelt to eat at the White House. There they met the President who "wanted to hear all about the day's events on Capitol Hill."

In the afternoon session, several of the youth congress leaders testified that their organization's membership included more than 4.5 million youths representing over sixty student and youth groups, but they denied that the American Youth Congress was "Communist-controlled." The following day, Joseph Lash, then the American Student Union's executive secretary, discussed his role in the movement before the committee. Afterward, Mrs. Roosevelt declared she had learned "nothing new," and once again invited the young people to the White House for lunch. Several days later, in her syndicated newspaper column, "My Day," she rebuked the committee's chief investigator, J. B. Mathews, stating, "His whole attitude . . . made one feel like a prisoner, considered guilty, being tried at the bar."

After the hearings ended, Mrs. Roosevelt publicly defended the American Youth Congress and her relationship to the organization. She declared she had investigated the group many years ago and had found "nothing to indicate any outside control." She stated that she knew many young people in the organization, had read most of the literature put out by the group, and had examined "all the resolutions passed at every meeting." "What else," she concluded, "can one do to keep from being duped?"

In May 1940, Mrs. Roosevelt agreed to speak to students at City College of New York. The Nazis had occupied the European Low Countries and were contesting the French. As she came through the main gate of the college, several members of the American Student Union shouted, "The Yanks are not coming." Mrs. Roosevelt replied, "All Right, all right, but what if the Nazis are?" This exchange signaled the beginning of a different relationship between Mrs. Roosevelt and the student activists. Her association with the student movement had been a strong and faithful one. In 1940, however, she finally lost patience especially after the American Youth Congress and American Student Union once again advocated an isolationist policy for the United States.

Although Mrs. Roosevelt had been enthusiastic between 1936 and 1939, when student organizations had praised the New Deal and supported preparedness, she now declared, "I don't think their present attitude is constructive," and added that she did not have time to work with a movement that did not have positive objectives. After the Nazi invasion of the Soviet Union in June 1941, when student leaders reversed themselves once more and urged that the United States take a strong stand against Hitler, Mrs. Roosevelt was highly skeptical of those youth congress leaders who again sought her support. In September, she wrote to them, "You seem to have forgotten conversations all of you had with me in the summer of 1940, and therefore do not realize the effect that your ... changed position ... since the invasion of Russia has had on me." While she remained as interested in the problems of youth as she had always been, she now began to seek new avenues for her concerns and energies.

It seems clear that Mrs. Roosevelt did not become involved in the student movement for political reasons. In fact, she had constantly rebuffed the President's advisors who cautioned her not to get involved because the students would "ask unpleasant and critical questions." She became interested in the youth movement because she cared about young people, especially those who were excited about politics. She wanted to make certain that they realized that the government was concerned about them. In May 1934, she declared she had "moments of real terror" when she thought "we may be losing this generation.... We have to make young people ... feel they are necessary."

In her dealings with the students, Mrs. Roosevelt seldom worried about the possibility that too many of them might have radical beliefs. Joseph Lash recalls, "To Eleanor, youth's radicalism was not a badge of untouchability but a plea for help and understanding." She was less afraid of militancy than of smugness and conformity. As for their radicalism, Mrs. Roosevelt often replied that the students were young, and would "outgrow it."

The activist who became the best friend of Eleanor Roosevelt and was also the most important student leader of the decade was Joseph Lash. In many ways what happened to Lash typifies the feelings and reactions of most students who were part of the movement. In the early 1930s, he was an ardent Socialist who supported a militant antiwar movement; by the end of the decade, he had become a New Deal liberal who opposed the Communist leadership of the national student organizations.

In February 1930, Joseph Lash was appointed to the managing board of the *Campus* at City College of New York, where he was an undergraduate; he had been a member of the newspaper's staff for nearly two years. In June 1931, Lash graduated from City College. The following year he became the editor of the *Student Outlook*, the monthly journal of the Student League for Industrial Democracy. In October a poem written by Lash appeared in the magazine. Entitled "Revolt," it symbolizes Lash's early radical views:

> Death of workers be a cyclone,
> Engulfing little winds of indecision.
> Impassioned sweep this land of opulence
> Smearing your prophecies of naked war
> On lofty lintels of aristocrats,
> For all their flags and genealogies.

Like other student leaders, Lash sought to extend the movement beyond the issue of peace. In 1932 he helped to organize a group of undergraduates and former students from ten eastern universities, which called itself the "Association of Unemployed College Alumni." Lash urged the students to propose legislation to Congress to cope with the nationwide problem of unemployment and help "eliminate its causes." He also attempted to unite the student movement with the labor movement. He declared that in order for the student movement to be successful it had to strike in labor's most crucial sectors: "Factory, mill, mine, and shop." Lash stated that he was disappointed that so little effort had been made in the yearly antiwar strikes to secure the support of organized labor, arguing that "such co-operation is absolutely vital to an effective strike against war."

During the height of the antiwar movement in 1934, Lash expressed the thoughts of most activists, when he wrote that there existed the growing conviction "that today war is more imminent than at any moment since 1918." He declared that most young people now realized that the First World War had not been fought "in behalf of the holy phrases advanced by the wartime statesmen, but was a struggle over markets, colonies, and spheres of influence."

In 1935, Lash was named the executive secretary of the Student League for Industrial Democracy. For several years he had argued against a united movement, because he believed that Socialists and Communists could not effectively work together. In December, however, when the merger between the National Student League and Student League for Industrial Democracy took place, Lash was enthusiastic. He hoped that the American Student Union would become a nonpolitical organization which would serve the interests of all students and avoid the polarization of the past. He was convinced that the April 1936 antiwar strike had helped to eliminate diversity among the activists. He stated that the strike "has become a juggernaut carrying before it the uncertain, the hesitant, [and] the sophistical."

By mid-1937 Lash was no longer an ardent Socialist; he now advocated that America adopt a foreign policy based on collective security. At the American Student Union convention in December, he favored dropping the Oxford pledge from the group's platform. "Our concern," he declared, "is with how to prevent war from spreading, . . the Oxford Pledge demobilizes the struggle for peace." He concluded that the pledge had kept "thousands of students out of the A.S.U.," because it "assumes that the main instigator of war today is the United States."

After leaving the Socialist party in late 1937, Lash drifted toward Communism. He participated in a Marxist study group, traveled to Spain where he "became an adherent of the Popular Front," and was considering accepting a job with the Communist newspaper, the *Daily Worker*, when in 1939 the announcement was made that the Soviets and Nazis had signed a nonaggression and trade pact. The union of Germany and Russia had a tremendous impact on Lash, as it did upon other activists who had supported the policies of the Soviet Union. He began to reevaluate most of his beliefs and views.

In November 1939, Lash, along with other youth leaders, was called before the House Committee on Un-American Activities. It was here that he "had his first serious encounter" with Eleanor Roosevelt, and moved away from his radical leanings. Most of the questions the committee asked Lash dealt with his views on the possibility of America working with the Russians for "democratic purposes." Lash stated that while he disagreed with the present position of the Communists in the American Student Union, it would be wrong to dissociate them from the organization, because the Communists "had worked hard and . . . have been cooperating with the forces of democracy." By the end of 1940, however, Lash believed it was no longer feasible to work with Communists for democratic goals.

It was while Lash was struggling to find a "third path" between Communism and Fascism that he developed his close friendship with Mrs. Roosevelt, a friendship that would last until her death. He has given credit to Mrs. Roosevelt for encouraging and supporting him during those difficult days. Mrs. Roosevelt, he stated, was "the single most important personal influence" in his transformation from radicalism to liberalism. Interestingly, Lash did not always feel this way about Mrs. Roosevelt. In early 1936, after she had invited several students, including Lash, to the White House to discuss the problems of youth, he observed that Mrs. Roosevelt was "a good woman utterly lacking in knowledge of social forces. . . . She was always sympathetic but helpless or sure that education alone could provide the solution."

In February 1941, the American Youth Congress demonstrated in Washington, D.C., for the last time. Its objective was to lobby against the proposed Lend-Lease act. Lash was permitted to speak in favor of the bill, and was greeted by "boos and hisses" when he approached the platform. He urged the youth congress to support the bill, and to remember that while England was not perfect, she was vastly preferable to Nazi Germany. As he left the podium, a youth congress member, who had been a college fraternity brother, hissed into Lash's ear: "Judas."

In 1942, Lash was again summoned to appear before the House Committee on Un-American Activities, and was asked why he had been a Communist. He explained that what had attracted him to Communism was not that liberals were moving toward Communism—a view held by many of the committee's members—but that he had believed that Communists were drifting closer to democracy. Prior to his appearance before the committee, Lash had sought a commission in the navy, but his application had been denied, a decision he attributed to his activities in the student movement. Several of the committee members suggested that his pursuit of a naval commission was designed to avoid the draft, and thus they sought to have his case reexamined. As a result, Lash's Selective Service classification was mysteriously transferred to 1-A, and on April 29, 1942, at the age of thirty-two, Joseph Lash was inducted into the army, where he served until October 1945.

Lash has compared his role in the student movement to revisiting an old love, who is hard to get along with and in the end betrays you, but you remember not the "misery and anguish," but the "glory and high romance of those days." He concluded that student activists did try "to make this a better world. And a surprisingly large number of us are still trying to do so."

Although undergraduates remained active between 1939 and 1941, these years are important primarily because they witnessed the continued decline in the intensity and popularity of the student movement. The two most significant developments, which culminated during this time, were that activists had finally to choose between stressing the benefits of peace or the horrors of the Nazis, and the involvement of Mrs. Roosevelt in the movement, which was responsible for influencing many youths to work with the government and forgo their radical beliefs for liberal ones.

8

REFLECTIONS AND CONCLUSIONS

The activities, protests, and confrontations involving thousands of activists during the 1930s were all part of America's first student movement. Students organized in large political groups and took part in nationwide efforts to alter existing conditions within the country. Although the experience of the thirties changed the nature of student activism in America, it is important to reflect upon the movement's limited scope. The various national student organizations never attracted many members. The largest number joined in 1939 when the American Student Union claimed twenty thousand members, although one observer has commented that only "12,000 were paid up," with the others being "sympathizers." (Iversen, p. 139.)

Moreover, the majority of students never took part in any event of the movement; the most being in 1936 when 350,000 students out of a college population of approximately 1,000,000—a degree of involvement, however, never equaled before or since—participated in the annual antiwar strike. There is certainly some truth in the observation, made in 1933 by writer Joseph Wood Krutch, that college students were much the same as they had always been. After visiting several Midwestern colleges, Krutch also declared that he found "no new spirit abroad, no changed attitude assumed toward a much changed world." He sadly concluded that "student bodies . . . are not rebellious, or cynical or even melancholy."

While Krutch may have oversimplified the situation, it should be reiterated that while the student movement dominated life on some campuses, with large numbers of undergraduates participating in its various activities, there existed thousands of students who were only remotely connected with these events. Many colleges would have echoed the response of administrators at Colorado State College to a questionnaire on student activism: There were no radical groups on campus and no "peace strike" or demonstration of any kind had taken place in either 1934 or 1935.

Similarly, the editors of the *Daily Nebraskan* reported an absence of student strikes at the University of Nebraska, and they expressed support for the "lethargic spirit" of the campus. Although New York City was a center of the movement, no students from Fordham, Manhattan, or St. Joseph's colleges participated in the antiwar strike of 1935. A student attending the University of Arizona returned to New York in the summer of 1935 and was amazed to read of the growing number of student revolts and strikes occurring at many universities. He observed that at Arizona "there is no political movement and never has been one." While some students were engaged in antiwar activity and in defending the abused civil liberties of their fellow undergraduates, many others would have identified more easily with the students at the University of Minnesota, who participated in the school's "pajama parade" in the spring of 1935. It was reported that more than three hundred male students "snake-danced" their way through the campus in "multicolored pajamas," ultimately breaking into several sorority houses.

A straw vote taken in October 1936 at the University of California, Berkeley—one of the more politically active campuses during the thirties—provides evidence that many college students were still inclined toward conservatism. The results of the presidential poll showed Alfred Landon, the Republican Party's candidate, defeating President Franklin D. Roosevelt, with Landon receiving 1,058 votes compared to Roosevelt's 952. Norman Thomas, the candidate of the Socialist Party, finished a distant third, with only 150 votes. In 1932, Herbert Hoover had received more than half the vote in a similar poll, with Norman Thomas edging Roosevelt for second. Thus while Roosevelt had improved his position greatly in four years, he did so more at the expense of the Socialists than of the Republicans. At best, one could say that the University of California, Berkeley, was still a conservative campus, with a significant minority of activists, although the school was less radical in 1936 than in 1932. On November 3, the editor of the *Daily Californian* declared that he was supporting Landon for President, stating that when he graduated he hoped "to work for a business concern," and that Landon's election would benefit business and consequently aid his chances "of getting a better job."

A poll conducted by the Institute of Public Opinion in 1936 revealed that college students were more conservative in their political views than were other persons of the same age. In a nationwide survey, the institute found that noncollege youths, by a ratio of 53 to 47 percent, favored granting Congress the power to regulate industry and agriculture, while college students polled opposed such action by a ratio of 54 to 46 percent. In January 1937, George Norlin, president of the University of Colorado, denied the claim that American universities were hotbeds of radicalism. He argued that most colleges were full of neither reactionaries, as charged by some activists, nor radicals, as asserted by William Randolph Hearst and others. Instead, Norlin contended that the great majority of colleges were "forward-looking institutions," but by their very nature were also "conserving institutions." He pointed out that at the University of Colorado, the majority of votes in the recent election for President of the United States went to Landon.

Many observers of the student movement perceived its limited features. After traveling around the country for four months talking to students, Maxine Davis, who wrote several books on America's youth, concluded that she found very few students ready to revolt. While agreeing that there were many student organizations in the country, she concluded that there "is no authentic youth movement." For the most part, Davis discovered that students meekly accepted "the fate meted out to them," and continued to believe "in a benign future based on wishful thinking." Hugh Miller, a professor of philosophy at the University of California, Los Angeles, in discussing whether there was a student movement in America, declared that there was a decided movement under way, but he observed that the difficulty with analyzing student and youth movements was that "there is so much motion and so little movement." (*Daily Bruin*, April 19, 1934.)

While a majority of students at most colleges were never personally involved in the movement, many undergraduates were familiar with some of the ideas and rhetoric which made up the political atmosphere on their campuses, a mood and tone set by the activists. In addition, the country's first politically inspired student movement existed in some form throughout the decade. The fact that hundreds of thousands of students participated in nationally organized demonstrations against American participation in war is in itself impressive, but it is even more significant because it occurred after a decade of student indifference to political life. As James Wechsler concluded in 1935, while most students may not have adopted any decisive stand, enormous inroads were made by the insurgents, and "anyone familiar with the American campus of a decade ago is astounded by the change in mood and interests."

The student movement of the 1930s was also in many ways a radical one. The leading student organizations were either Socialist- or Communist-oriented, with their members strongly critical of the established ideals underpinning American society. Moreover, the activities, attitudes, and behavior of the student activists—at least, prior to 1936—can best be described as militant. Large-scale strikes and confrontations with university officials were a radical departure from traditional forms of college protest. The concept of mass student demonstrations, which culminated in the antiwar strikes, had its inception early in the decade, with the Reed Harris incident. No university or college had ever before witnessed such massive dissent, and students at other institutions, faced with similar situations, adopted the procedures established at Columbia. Those methods and techniques seem tame today, but in the thirties, they represented a bold and unprecedented step.

The most successful and publicized event of the student movement—the antiwar strike—was also its most militant. While there was no attempt to "shut down" a university or "take over" an administration building, the strikes were called for eleven o'clock—one of the busier hours for any college—and the participants walked out of their assigned classes, rather than merely not attending them. Furthermore, the speakers who addressed the striking students did not embark upon maudlin elicitations of the virtues of peace or in rationalizations of their country's involvement in the First World War. James Wechsler noted that activists did not "fly the dove of peace," nor place faith "in the divine benevolence of statesmen." For the most part, angry and determined students listened to such speakers as Earl Browder and Norman Thomas condemn imperialism, war, and America's military expenditures, and participated in demonstrations that were sanctioned neither by university administrations nor undergraduate student councils. Strikers would often leave the campus and march into nearby communities to voice their concerns. Students did not engage in these activities because they sought to foment trouble or violence; they acted because they believed in the seriousness and immediacy of the war threat.

Student leaders were clearly aware of the militant connotation of the word "strike." The editors of the *Student Outlook* maintained that the term was selected because everyone recognized that it represented "the most intensive form of protest." They pointed out that while conferences and symposiums seldom were mentioned in the press, the 1934 Student Strike Against War made "column 1, page 1, of the New York *Times*, and started discussions on hundreds of campuses." Hal Draper declared that all year long students listened to speakers explain the causes of war, but "on Strike Day we *act*." One participant concluded that the student strike was "a demonstration of power," showing activists that they could "make an impression." Others observed that the most significant aspect of the strike "is the sight of hundreds of thousands of students rising simultaneously in every part of the country."

Student leaders believed that the strike was the key to the entire movement. James Wechsler and Joseph Lash both stated that no other gesture "more accurately reflects the temper of the student peace movement." They argued that the strike was the most "potent instrument that students can employ . . . to curtail war preparations, combat compulsory military training, and prevent a specific war situation." Lash declared that the strike had a cohesive force, which wove "a bond of solidarity from campus to campus. . . . This feeling of solidarity has marked the crystallization of the student movement in America."

At many colleges, the movement achieved a success far greater than seemed possible with its small numbers. At Vassar, the editorial staff of the school's newspaper, the *Miscellany News*, was made up of members of the American Student Union chapter. At Hunter College, the entire American Student Union slate of candidates, which ran on a platform of total support for the Student Strike Against War, was elected to office in 1936. At Reed College in Oregon, American Student Union members included the president of the student council, the president of the freshman class, the editor of the campus newspaper, and a majority of the student council members. The *Student Advocate* reported in October 1936 that American Student Union slates in five colleges "have swept the student council elections, . . . and the majority of college papers are edited by A.S.U. people."

Prior to 1932, the student government at the University of Virginia was in control of the college's fraternities. In the fall of 1932, however, a student named Chance Stoner established a Marxist study class. He "organized the rest of the student body," became its president, and rewrote the college's constitution. In 1935 he led Virginia's first antiwar strike, which "shut down all university classes." In the fall of 1936, a course on the "cause, cost, and consequences of war" was offered for the first time at Dartmouth College. Its objective was to study the nature of war and the obstacles that prevented peace from being established. The creation of the course was the result of a petition signed by the members of the student government and a general vote of the entire student body supporting that petition during the antiwar strike of April 1936.

The student movement was an early casualty of the Second World War, but its impact remained. The movement had jarred but not shattered the tradition of political apathy that existed on most campuses across America. More important, it established the sort of militant activism which would be expanded by students a generation later. The authors of various studies on student activism have concluded that many of the protestors of the 1960s were children of those who had been the student radicals of the 1930s. In addition, it would seem that the student movement provided a training ground for many of the political and intellectual leaders in postwar society. It was during the turmoil of the thirties that the liberal spokesmen of the fifties learned to make speeches, organize their associates, and battle the establishment. As Hal Draper has observed, the history of the student movement of the thirties is one of "the most important educational institutions of twentieth-century America."

BIBLIOGRAPHY

STUDENT NEWSPAPERS, JOURNALS, HANDBILLS, ETC.

Academic Front (journal of the Communist Party Unit), University of California, Berkeley, December 1935-March 1938.
Alumni News (publication of the Alumni Association), Columbia University, 1929-1941.
American Youth Act (pamphlet of the American Youth Congress), New York, 1935.
The Anti-War Movement of the Students of the University of California, March-April, 1935 (pamphlet), University of California, Berkeley, 1935.
The Archive (monthly publication by graduate students), Duke University, 1932-1936.
Bulletin, New York University, 1934-1941.
Bulletin, of the Anti-Fascist Association of City College of New York (weekly publication), City College of New York, 1934-1935.
Campus, City College of New York, 1921-1941.
City College Alumnus (publication of the Alumni Association), City College of New York, 1930-1941.
Communist Companile (journal of the Young Communist League), University of California, Berkeley, 1935-1943.
Daily Bruin, University of California, Los Angeles, 1927-1941.
Daily Californian, University of California, Berkeley, 1921-1941.
Daily News, New York University, 1925-1933.
Daily Trojan, University of Southern California, 1930-1941.
Faculty Bulletin (weekly publication), City College of New York, 1931-1935.
Liberal Arts College Bulletin (monthly publication of the Liberal Arts College Movement), Westminster, Maryland, November 1930-September 1932.
Microcosm (undergraduate publication), City College of New York, 1931-1935.
New Student (periodical of the Intercollegiate Liberal League), New York, 1922-1929.
Newsletter (publication of the American Youth Congress), New York, 1935-1939.
Occident (literary magazine), University of California, Berkeley, 1930-1941.
Ohio State Monthly (published by the Ohio State University Association), Ohio State University, 1931-1937.

Report of Proceedings, American Student Union, Fourth National Convention, (December 27-30, 1938). The official report of the convention held at City College of New York.
Sather Gate Handbills (literature distributed by various student organizations), University of California, Berkeley, March 1935-December 1941.
Spectator, Columbia University, 1927-1941.
Student (underground student publication), City College of New York, September 1932-February 1935.
Student Advocate (journal of the American Student Union), New York, February 1936-March 1938.
Student Almanac (pamphlet of the American Student Union), New York, 1939.
Student Outlook (journal of the Student League for Industrial Democracy), New York, October 1932-October 1935.
Student Outpost (journal of the Social Problems Club), University of California, Berkeley, February 1932-November 1935.
Student Review (journal of the National Student League), New York, December 1931-October 1935.
Student Socialist (publication of the Young People's Socialist League), University of California, Berkeley, September 1939-January 1940.
Students' Rights Association Bulletin (undergraduate publication), University of California, Berkeley, November 27, 1934.
Students Take a Stand: An Account of Student Conferences During Christmas Week, 1933 (publication of the National Student League), University of California, Berkeley, 1934.
Washington State Evergreen, Washington State College, May 1936.
Young Communist League: Handbills Distributed at the University of California by the Young Communist League, 1935-1949, University of California, Berkeley.
Young Socialists: Handbills Distributed by Socialist Organizations at the University of California, 1936-1951, University of California, Berkeley.

ARTICLES AND PERIODICALS

The articles written by the participants in the movement and those that describe the student demonstrations and protests of the 1930s were the most helpful.

Adler, Mortimer J. "This Pre-War Generation: Our College Students and Recent Graduates Recognize No Moral Issues," *Harper's,* CLXXI (October 1940), 524-534.
"Admission of Unemployed Students to the University of Minnesota," *School and Society,* XXIX (January 6, 1934), 9.
Akeley, Evelyn. "Study of Student Aid Under the N.Y.A.," *School and Society,* L (November 25, 1939), 701-704.
"Among American Students Half Blame Germany for War," *Science News Letter,* XXXVII (March 2, 1940), 141.
"At the Observation Post: College Rah-Rah Era Passing into History," *Literary Digest,* CXIX (March 16, 1935), 11.
Bain, Read. "Changed Beliefs of College Students," *Journal of Abnormal and Social Psychology,* XXXI (April 1936), 1-11.
Bliven, Bruce, Jr. "Citizens of Tomorrow," *New Republic,* XCVII (January 11, 1939), 283.
Boldt, W. J., and J. B. Stroud. "Changes in the Attitudes of College Students," *Journal of Educational Psychology,* XXV (November 1934), 611-619.
Boroff, David. "A Kind of Proletarian Harvard," *New York Times Magazine* (March 28, 1965), 29, 106-109.
Brameld, Theodore B. "College Students React to Social Issues," *Frontiers of Democracy,* I (November 1934), 21-26.

112 / BIBLIOGRAPHY

Breemes, E. L., H. H. Remmers, and C. L. Morgan. "Changes in Liberalism—Conservatism of College Students Since the Depression," *Journal Of Social Psychology*, XIV (1941), 99-107.

Buck, Walter. "A Measurement of Changes in Attitudes and Interests of University Students Over a Ten-Year Period," *Journal of Abnormal and Social Psychology*, XXXI (April 1936), 12-19.

Bulletin, American Friends Service Committee (1930-1940).

Bulletin, of The American Association of University Professors, XX-XIV (1934-1938).

Carlson, Hilding B. "Attitudes of Undergraduate Students," *Journal of Social Psychology*, V (May 1934), 202-213.

"Catholic Students Are Against War," *Christian Century*, LVI (November 22, 1939), 1428.

"College Poll on War," *Nation*, CXXXVI (May 24, 1933), 571.

"College Students vs. the ROTC," *Survey*, LXX (May, 1934), 168.

Comstock, Alzada. "The College Girl: 1933 Model," *Current History*, XXXIX (November 1933), 180-184.

Draper, Hal. "The American Student Union Faces the Student Anti-War Strike," *American Socialist Monthly*, V (April 1936), 7-12.

Dudycha, George J. "The Moral Beliefs of College Students," *International Journal of Ethics*, XLIII (1933), 194-204.

"Enrollments Zoom at U.S. Colleges," *Literary Digest*, CXXII (October 17, 1936), 38.

Erber, Ernest. "The Yipsel Convention," *Socialist Appeal*, I, 5 (August-September 1935), 16-18.

Farnsworth, Paul R. "Changes in 'Attitude toward War' during the College Years," *Journal of Social Psychology*, VIII (1937), 274-279.

Foster, William T. "Is There an American Youth Movement," *National Student Mirror*, I (March 1934), 3-5.

Fowler, C. "Youth Ticket," *New Outlook*, CLXV (January 1935), 39-42.

Goldman, Albert. "Toward Socialist Clarity," *Socialist Appeal*, II, 3 (January-February 1936), 7-8.

Graham, Edward K. "The Hampton Institute Strike of 1927: A Case Study in Student Protest," *The American Scholar*, XXXVIII (Autumn 1969), 668-682.

"Great Boom in Student Drinking," *Literary Digest*, CXXIII (March 6, 1937), 3-6.

Hamilton, Al, and Alvaine Hollister. "Left Jingoism on the Campus," *Socialist Review*, VI (January-February 1938), 9-10, 19.

Harrison, Lowell H. "Rowdies, Riots, and Rebellions," *American History Illustrated*, VII, 3 (June 1972), 18-29.

Hibbard, Addison. "Out Truant Professors," *Outlook*, CL (December 5, 1928), 1267-1269.

"Hopkins Answers Critics of Federal Aid for Students," *Newsweek*, IV (December 1, 1934), 38.

"Is There a Student Movement in America?" *New Republic*, LXXXI (January 6, 1935), 264.

Johnson, D. G., and M. M. Willey. "Backgrounds of College N.Y.A. Students," *School and Society*, L (August 19, 1939), 252-256.

Krutch, Joseph Wood. "What Does the Younger Generation Think?" *Nation*, CXLI (July 24, 1935), 697-698.

Lash, Joseph P. "Another View of the American Student Union," *American Socialist Monthly*, V (May 1936), 28-31.

———. "The Student Strike," *Fellowship*, II (May 1936), 5-6.

———. "Unemployed College Graduates, Call for Legislative Action," *Nation*, CXXXVI (April 12, 1933), 408.

Laski, Harold. "Why Don't Your Young Men Care?" *Harper's*, CLXIII (July 1931), 129-136.

"Laying the Ghost of College Communism," *Literary Digest,* CXX (July 27, 1935), 18.
Lee, Jennie. "A Diary from a Kentucky Mining Camp," *World Tomorrow,* XV (March 1932), 83-84.
Magnes, Judah L. "A Tragic Dilemma," *Christian Century,* LVII (March 22, 1940), 406-407.
McDowell, Arthur G. "The Socialist Youth Movement," *American Socialist Quarterly,* III, 2 (Summer 1934), 43-50.
Meyers, Robin. "War and Peace on the Campus," *Socialist Review,* VI (May-June 1939), 11-13.
Most, Melos. "Militancy Comes of Age in the Young People's Socialist League," *Socialist Appeal,* I, 5 (August-September 1935), 12-15.
"Naive-Neckers: Stanford Students Split in Necking-Petting Questionnaire," *Literary Digest,* CCXXIII (March 20, 1937), 30-31.
Neblett, Thomas F. "Youth Movements in the United States," American Academy of Political and Social Science *Annals,* CXCIV (November 1937), 141-151.
Nelson, Erland. "Radicalism-Conservatism in Student Attitudes," *Psychological Monographs,* L, 4 (1938), 1-32.
"No Students on the Barricades: College Students and Politics," *Outlook and Independent,* CLX (January 6, 1932), 9.
Norlin, George. "Is Radicalism Rampant on the American College Campus?" *School and Society,* XLVI (January 23, 1937), 120-122.
"Oath Bill Defeated—New York State," *Literary Digest,* CXIX (March 23, 1935), 18.
Peterson, Patti Mc Gill. "Student Organizations and the Antiwar Movement in America, 1900-1960," *American Studies,* XIII, 1 (Spring 1972), 131-147.
Pihlblad, Carl T. "Student Attitudes Toward War," *Sociology and Social Research,* XX (January 1936), 248-254.
Porter, Kenneth Wiggins. "The Oxford-Caps War at Harvard," *New England Quarterly,* XIV (March 1941), 77-83.
"Queer Doings in the Northwest: Dismissal of Dr. Fisher," *New Republic,* IC (June 28, 1939), 199.
Ross, Irwin. "College Students and the War," *New Republic,* CIII (July 15, 1940), 79-80.
Seeley, Evelyn. "Varied Glimpses of the Collegiate Mind," *Literary Digest,* CXIX (Mary 25, 1935), 22-24.
Seidman, Harold. "How Radical Are College Students?" *The American Scholar,* V (Summer 1935), 326-330.
"Sit-Down Strikes: Campus Strikes Cover Varied Complaints," *Literary Digest,* CXXIII (March 27, 1937), 29-30.
Sowards, Genevieve S. "A Study of the War Attitudes of College Students," *Journal of Abnormal and Social Psychology,* XXIX (October 1934), 328-333.
Sproul, R. G. "Universities Face Radicalism," *Rotarian,* XLV (October 1934), 22-24.
"Strike of Students of Journalism at the State University of Louisiana," *School and Society,* XL (December 8, 1934), 766.
"Striking for Warless World: American College Students Schedule Parades," *Literary Digest,* CXXI (April 11, 1936), 35.
"Student Aid Under the N.Y.A.," *School and Society,* XLII (November 2, 1935), 597.
"Student Interests at Harvard University," *School and Society,* (October 19, 1935), 528-529.
"Student Pacifists Organize," *Fellowship,* III (December, 1937), 8.
"Student Revolt," *Literary Digest,* CX (July 4, 1931), 22.
"Student Strike Against War," *Literary Digest,* CXVII (April 28, 1934), 38.
"Student Strike Against War," *Literary Digest,* CXIX (March 23, 1935), 17.

114 / BIBLIOGRAPHY

"Students and Communism: Dies Committee Airs Charges, Mrs. Roosevelt Looks On," *Newsweek*, XIV (December 11, 1939), 53-54.
"Students in Kentucky," *New Republic*, LXX (April 20, 1932), 267.
"Students Wage Vegetable War to End War," *Newsweek*, III (April 21, 1934), 34.
Thornbury, Ethel. "Witch-Hunters at Work: Wisconsin," *New Republic*, LXXXIII (June 19, 1935), 158-159.
"A Tragic Dilemma," *Christian Century*, LVII (March 27, 1940), 406-407.
"Two Presidents Urge Less Relief, Better Standards," *Newsweek*, IV (November 17, 1934), 4.
Tyler, August. "The International Socialist Youth Movement," *American Socialist Quarterly*, II, 1 (Winter 1933), 49-56.
Wallace, Anna. "Fascism Comes to the Campus," *New Republic*, LXXXI (January 9, 1935), 238-241.
Wallace, Henry A. "The Potentialities of the Youth Movement in America," *Educational Record*, XV (January, 1934), 3-9.
Walters, Raymond. "Statistics of Registration in American Universities and Colleges," *School and Society*, XXXII-L (December 13, 1930-December 16, 1939).
Wechsler, James A. "Ferment in the Colleges," *New Republic*, LXXXIV (October 1935), 266-268.
Weyl, Nathaniel. "College in Rebellion," *New Republic*, LXXIII (November 16, 1932), 73.
Wieman, Henry N., and Arthur E. Holt. "Keep Our Country Out of This War," *Christian Century*, LVI (March 1939), 1163.
Wilkens, Ernest H. "Shall We Sign the Pacifist Pledge? No," *Christian Century*, LII (December 11, 1935), 1586-1588.
Yates, Dorothy H. "How the Depression and Its Consequences Have Affected Teachers, College Students," *School and Society*, XXXIX (May 5, 1934), 571-574.
"Youth in College," *Fortune*, XIII (June 1936), 99-102, 153-162.
"Youth Votes for Peace," *Nation*, CXXXIV (January 27, 1932), 91.

BOOKS

The most important works were those written by the activists, especially the books by Joseph P. Lash and James Wechsler. Although the various aspects of education have long interested scholars, the majority of the books on student activism either lack sophisticated analysis or are concerned with a sociological examination of the protest of the 1960s. Moreover, no author since Wechsler in 1935 has devoted an entire study to the student movement of the thirties.

Alexander, Charles C. *Nationalism in American Thought, 1930-1945*. Chicago, 1969. The best social and cultural history of the period.
Allmendinger, David F., Jr. *Paupers and Scholars: The Transformation of Student Life in New England, 1760-1860*. New York, 1975. A provocative new interpretation of student unrest prior to the Civil War.
Beale, Howard K. *Are American Teachers Free? An Analysis of the Restraints Upon the Freedom of Teaching in American Schools*. New York, 1936.
Bell, Daniel. "The Background and Development of Marxian Socialism in the United States," in Donald Drew Egbert and Stow Persons, eds., *Socialism and American Life*. Vol. I. Princeton, 1952, pp. 215-405.
Bell, Howard M. *Youth Tell Their Story*. Washington, D.C., 1938.
Birnbaum, Norman, and Marjorie Childers. "The American Student Movement," in Julian Nagel, ed., *Student Power*. London, 1969, pp. 125-141.
Bronson, Walter C. *The History of Brown University, 1764-1914*. Providence, R.I., 1914.

Brubaker, John S., and Willis Rudy. *Higher Education in Transition.* New York, 1958.
Cantril, Hadley, ed. *Public Opinion, 1935-1946.* Princeton, 1951.
Carter, Dan T. *Scottsboro: A Tragedy of the American South.* Baton Rouge, 1969.
Chatfield, Charles. *For Peace and Justice: Pacifism in America, 1914-1941.* Knoxville, Tenn., 1971.
Davis, Maxine. *The Lost Generation.* New York, 1936.
Douglas, Frederick. *Life and Times of Frederick Douglas.* rev. ed. New York, 1962.
Draper, Hal. "The Student Movement of the Thirties," in Rita James Simon, ed., *As We Saw the Thirties: Essays on Social and Political Movements of a Decade.* Urbana, Ill., 1967, pp. 151-189. A rambling, disjointed essay by one of the more militant activists of the 1930s.
Earnest, Ernest. *Academic Procession: An Informal History of the American College, 1636 to 1953.* Indianapolis, 1953.
Ellsworth, Frank, and Martha Burns. *Student Activism in American Higher Education.* Washington, D.C., 1970.
Fass, Paula S. *The Damned and the Beautiful: American Youth in the 1920s.* New York, 1978.
Feldman, Kenneth A., and Theodore A. Newcomb. *The Impact of College on Students: An Analysis of Four Decades of Research.* San Francisco, 1969.
Feuer, Lewis S. *The Conflict of Generations: The Character and Significance of Student Movements.* New York, 1969. The most extensive research by any author on student protest. Unfortunately, Feuer's refusal to recognize pluralistic motivations for student unrest mars his judgments.
Gallup, George. *The Gallup Poll: Public Opinion, 1935-1971.* 3 vols. New York, 1972. Vol. I; *1935-1948.*
Harrington, Michael. *Socialism.* New York, 1972.
Hatchly, Louis C. *The History of Bowdoin College.* Portland, Me., 1929.
Howe, Irving, and Lewis Coser. *The American Communist Party: A Critical History.* New York, 1962.
Ickes, Harold L. *The Secret Diary of Harold L. Ickes.* 3 vols. New York, 1954. Vol. III: *The Lowering Clouds, 1939-1941.*
Iversen, Robert. *The Communists and the Schools.* New York, 1959.
Katz, Daniel, and Floyd H. Allport. *Students' Attitudes.* Syracuse, N.Y., 1931.
Kazin, Alfred. *Starting Out in the Thirties.* Boston, 1962.
Kerr, Clark. "Student Dissent and Confrontation Politics," in Julian Foster and Darwood Long, eds., *Protest! Student Activism in America.* New York, 1970, pp. 3-10.
Kinsey, Alfred C., et al. *Sexual Behavior in the Human Female.* Philadelphia. 1953.
Krieg, James C. "City College of New York, 1932-1934: The Radicalization of the University." Senior thesis, Princeton University, 1971.
Lash, Joseph P. *The Campus: A Fortress of Democracy.* New York, 1937. A report of the third annual convention of the American Student Union.
———. Letter to the author. February 25, 1974.
———. *The Campus Strikes Against War.* New York: Student League for Industrial Democracy, n.d. (1935).
———. *Eleanor and Franklin.* New York, 1971.
———. *Eleanor Roosevelt: A Friend's Memoir.* New York, 1964.
Lawson, Alan R. *The Failure of Independent Liberalism, 1930-1941.* New York, 1971.
Lee, Calvin B. T. *The Campus Scene: 1900-1970.* New York, 1970. A highly general but interesting account of student life in the United States during the twentieth century.
Lewack, Harold. *Campus Rebels: A Brief History of the Student League for Industrial Democracy.* New York: Student League for Industrial Democracy, 1953.

Lindley, Betty and Ernest K. *A New Deal for Youth: The Story of the National Youth Administration.* New York, 1938.
Lipset, Seymour M., and Gerald M. Schaflander. *Passion and Politics: Student Activism in America.* Boston, 1971. A useful sociological examination of student protest.
Lord, John King. *A History of Dartmouth College.* Concord, N. H. 1913.
MacLennan, Hugh. "What it was Like to be in Your Twenties in the Thirties," in Victor Hoar, ed., *The Great Depression.* New York, 1969, pp. 144-155.
McGill, Nettie P., and Ellen N. Matthews. *The Youth of New York City.* New York, 1940.
Morison, Samuel Eliot. *Three Centuries of Harvard, 1636-1936.* Cambridge, Mass. 1936.
Murphy, Gardner, and Rensis Likert. *Public Opinion and the Individual: A Psychological Study of Student Attitudes on Public Questions, with a Retest Five Years Later.* New York, 1938.
Newcomb, Theodore M. *Personality and Social Change.* New York, 1943.
Orum, Anthony M., ed. *The Seeds of Politics: Youth and Politics in America.* New Jersey, 1972.
Peckham, Howard H. *The Making of the University of Michigan: 1817-1967.* Ann Arbor, 1967.
Peterson, George E. *The New England College in the Age of the University.* Amherst, 1964.
Rawick, George P. "The New Deal and Youth: The Civilian Conservation Corps, the National Youth Administration, and the American Youth Congress." Ph.D. dissertation, University of Wisconsin, 1957. The dissertation is primarily a study of the two leading government agencies that were involved with the problems of youth. Rawick actually was more interested in the battles between the Communist and Socialist members of the American Youth Congress than in developing the story of the student movement.
Richmond, Al. *A Long View from the Left: Memoirs of an American Revolutionary.* Boston, 1973.
Roosevelt, Elliott, ed. *F. D. R.: His Personal Letters, 1928-1945.* 2 vols. New York, 1950.
Rosenman, Samuel I., comp. *The Public Papers and Addresses of Franklin D. Roosevelt.* 13 vols. New York, 1938-50.
Rudy, Willis. *The College of the City of New York: A History, 1847-1947.* New York, 1949.
Sagendorph, Kent. *Michigan: The Story of the University.* New York, 1948.
Steffins, Lincoln. *The Autobiography of Lincoln Steffins.* New York, 1931.
Studenski, Paul. *Liquor Consumption Among American Youth: A Study of the Drinking Habits of Certain Segments of American Youth.* New York, 1937.
Susman, Warren I. "The Thirties," in Stanley Coben and Lorman Ratner, eds., *The Development of an American Culture.* New Jersey, 1970, pp. 179-218.
Terkel, Studs. *Hard Times.* New York, 1970.
Tyler, William S. *History of Amherst College During its First Half Century, 1821-1871.* Springfield, Mass., 1873.
Wechsler, James A. *The Age of Suspicion.* New York, 1953.
———. *Revolt on the Campus.* New York, 1935. Although it must be read with caution, since the author was eager to gain recruits for the movement, the book captures the mood and intensity of the activists of the thirties.
——— and Joseph P. Lash. *War Our Heritage.* New York, 1936.
Wittner, Lawrence. *Rebels Against War: The American Peace Movement 1941-1960.* New York, 1969.

INDEX

Addams, Jane, 30, 60
Adler, Mortimer J., 90-91
Albers, Edna, 49
Albion College, 11
Alumni News, 9
Amalgamated Clothing Workers Union, 74
American Association of University Professors, 15, 63
American Civil Liberties Union, 21, 41
American Communist party, 58-60, 70-71, 76, 87, 95
American Federation of Labor, 68
American Friends Service Committee, 29
American League against War and Fascism, 60, 70, 72
American Legion, 72
American Student Union, 9, 29, 58, 69, 72-74, 77-93, 96, 98-99, 101-102, 104, 108
American University, 42
American Youth Act, 68, 80, 84, 96
American Youth Congress, 67-69, 77, 80-81, 84, 86, 88, 91-93, 95-100, 102
Amherst University, 3-4, 36
Anti-War Club, 87
Archive, The, 45
Argo, 5
Association of Unemployed College Alumni, 101
Atkinson, Thomas, 64

Barnes, Harry Elmer, 55
Barometer, 7
Beale, Howard K., 49
Beard, Charles A., 32
Beichman, Arnold, 12
Bell, Howard M., 14
Boldt, W. J., 14
Boston University, 32, 95
Bowdoin University, 4
Brameld, Theodore B., 14
Breemes, E. L., 14
Brooklyn College, 42, 93
Broun, Heywood, 58
Browder, Earl, 59, 107
Brown University, 3-4, 16, 57
Bryn Mawr, 65
Buck, Walter, 7
Bulletin, 73, 81
Butler, Nicholas Murray, 7, 25, 43

Campbell, Jeffrey, 86
Campus, 10, 32, 52-53, 73, 75, 80, 92-93, 100
Carthage College, 63
Chautauquas, 74
City College of New York, 19, 24-26, 29, 32-38, 40-42, 46, 48, 58, 61, 64, 74-75, 80, 84, 87, 90-91, 98-100
Civilian Conservation Corps, 68, 91
Clancy, Robert, 9
Coal Miners' Strike (Harlan County), 21-22, 25, 35, 74
Cohen, Felix, 32
Colby College, 80
Collective security, 78-79, 81-83, 86-89, 91-95, 101

118 / INDEX

College of the Ozarks, 42
Colorado State College, 105
Columbia University, 7, 9, 11, 14, 19, 21-26, 30-31, 38, 40, 42-43, 52, 58, 64, 78-79, 81, 107
Committee for the Recognition of Classroom Generals, 90
Comstock, Alzada, 6-7
Congress, U.S., 55, 68, 80-81, 84, 96-97, 101, 106
Congress of Industrial Organizations, 74, 97
Connecticut Valley Student Conference against War, 36
Coolidge, Calvin, 5
Cornell University, 31, 43
Crane, A. G., 7
Cummings, E. E., 55

Daily Bruin, 9, 12, 33, 39, 44, 57
Daily Californian, 33, 39, 45, 48-49, 73, 105
Daily Illini, 44
Daily Maroon, 12, 30
Daily Nebraskan, 105
Daily News, 16, 33
Daily Princetonian, 43, 56
Daily Texan, 12
Daily Worker, 60, 102
Daniell, Eugene S., 38
Darrow, Clarence, 20
Dartmouth University, 3, 36, 108
Daughters of the American Revolution, 81
Davis, Maxine, 8, 106
Declaration of Rights of American Youth, 68
Dennett, Tyler, 65
Depression, 6, 12-14, 18, 27, 58-59, 61, 63-66
Detroit Board of Education, 52
Dewey, John, 32
Dodds, Harold, 47
Douglas, Melvyn, 98
Drake University, 64
Draper, Hal, 79, 93-94, 107, 109
Dudycha, George, 8
Duke University, 38, 45, 48

Edwards, George, 72, 79
Einstein, Albert, 30-31
Emergency Peace Campaign, 94
Englebrecht, Helmuth C., 55

Fabor, Harold, 84
Federal Emergency Relief Administration, 65

Feuer, Lewis S., 19
Fisher, Charles H., 27
Food Workers Industrial Union, 74
Fordham College, 105
Fortune, 8, 55
Franco, Francisco, 82
Frank, Glenn, 64
Franklin and Marshall College, 91
Fresno State College, 44

Gallup poll, 8, 50, 54
Gauss, Christian, 47
Gibbs, Philip, 55
Goucher College, 74
Gratton, C. Hartley, 55

Hall, Rob, 22
Hamilton, Al, 86
Hampton Institute, 52
Hardeman, D. B., 12
Harris, Reed, 22-24, 26, 48, 107
Harvard University, 3-4, 13, 19, 21, 37, 90, 97
Hearst, William Randolph, 50, 52-53, 106
Hebrew University, 95
Hemingway, Ernest, 55
Henderson, Donald, 25-26
Hibbard, Addison, 20
Hinckley, William, 81
Hitler, Adolf, 19, 37, 52, 54-55, 67, 75, 80, 94-95, 100
Holland, E. O., 51
Hollister, Alvaine, 83, 86
Hoover, Herbert, 15, 105
Hopkins, Harry, 65
House Committee on Un-American Activities, 60, 98-99, 102-103
Howard University, 31, 42, 52, 65
Humphrey, Herman, 4
Hunt, W. T., 10
Hunter College, 38, 42, 84, 108

Ilma, Viola, 67-68, 98
Independent Socialist League, 93
Institute of Public Opinion, 105
Intercollegiate Disarmament Council, 16, 32
Intercollegiate Liberal League, 5
Intercollegiate Socialist Society, 20
International Defense Fund, 76
Isolationism, 87, 92, 97, 99

Jacobucci, Joseph, 48
Jingo Day, 34
John Hopkins University, 38

INDEX / 119

Johnson, Arnold, 21
Johnson, Oakley, 24-26

Kansas State College, 80
Kazin, Alfred, 61
Kerr, Clark, 18
Kinsey, Alfred, 6
Krutch, Joseph Wood, 104
Ku Klux Klan, 27, 70, 98
Kutztown State Teachers College, 91

LaFollette, Robert, 5
Laidler, Harry, 20
Landon, Alfred, 105-106
Lane Theological Seminary, 4
Lantern, 76
Lash, Joseph, 56, 60, 71-72, 79, 83-85, 92, 97, 99-103, 108
Laski, Harold, 27
Lasswell, Harold, 55
Lawson, Alan, 94
League for Political Education, 62
Lend-Lease, 102
Lenin, Nikolai, 59
Lerner, Max, 22
Lewis, John L., 74, 84, 97
Liberal Arts College Bulletin, 63
Likert, Rensis, 14
Lippman, Walter, 97
Lipset, Seymour M., 6
Literary Digest, 9-10, 56
London, Jack, 20
Long, Huey P., 43, 49
Louisiana State University, 48-49, 64
Lovett, Robert Morss, 50

MacArthur, Douglas, 47
MacLennan, Hugh, 54
Macquarrie, T. W., 43
Magnes, Judah, 95
Manhattan College, 105
Marx, Karl, 59
Mathews, J. B., 60, 99
Matthews, Ellen N., 13
McCarthy, Joseph, 60
McGill, Nettie P., 13
McMichael, Jack, 99
McNutt, Waldo, 67
Mencken, H. L., 58
Merriman, Robert B., 97
Michael Mullins Chowder and Marching Club, 37
Middlebury College, 5
Miller, Hugh, 106
Millis, Walter, 55, 94
Minnesota Daily, 44

Miscellany News, 108
Moore, Ernest C., 38-39, 40, 43
Moore, Justin, 48
Morehouse College, 52
Morgan, C. L., 14
Morgan, J. P., 52
Morison, Samuel Eliot, 3
Mount Holyoke College, 6, 10
Murphy, Gardner, 14
Murrish, Bill, 49
Mussolini, Benito, 40, 52, 54-55

National Association for the Advancement of Colored People, 76
National Conference on Students and Politics, 32, 70
National Council of Student Christian Associations, 32
National Interfraternity Conference, 81
National Student Federation, 31, 62, 66-67, 77
National Student League, 20-22, 24, 26, 28-29, 31-32, 36-40, 43, 46, 56-59, 69-74, 76-77, 79, 88, 101
National Student Mirror, 67
National Youth Administration, 65-66, 68-69, 72, 77, 80, 84, 98
Nazi-Soviet pact, 92
Neal, John R., 24
Nelson, Erland, 16
Neutrality Act, 85
New Deal, 67, 78, 80, 84-85, 89, 92, 99-100
New International, The, 93
New Republic, 34, 57
New Student, 5
New York City Board of Education, 49
New York *Herald Tribune,* 50, 91
New York *Post,* 41
New York State Model Youth Legislature, 98
New York Student League, 20
New York *Times,* 107
New York University, 4, 20, 31, 45, 52, 64, 71, 81, 83-84, 93
Newcomb, Theodore, 15
Newman, Walter, 45
Niebuhr, Reinhold, 32, 38
Norlin, George, 106
Nunan-Devaney bill, 49-50
Nye Committee, 55

Oberlin College, 4-5
Occident, 10
Office of Education, U.S., 63, 67

Ohio State Monthly, 43, 64
Ohio State University, 16, 20, 32-33, 43, 64, 72, 76
Olympic games, 1936, 67, 75
Oregon State University, 7
Orum, Anthony, 18
Outlook and Independent, 19
Oxford pledge, 37, 47, 52, 72, 78-80, 83, 98, 101-102

Phillips College, 42
Pihlbald, Carl T., 16
Popular Front, 70, 79, 95, 102
Princeton University, 3, 19, 47, 52, 54, 66
Purdue University, 10, 14

Rankin, Jeannette, 42
Rawick, George, 93
Reed College, 108
Remarque, Erick, 55
Remmers, H. H., 14
Reserve Officers' Training Corps, 22, 30-34, 36-38, 42, 46-49, 67, 71-72, 80, 82, 91
Revolt, 28
Reynolds, Agnes, 85, 92
Richmond, Al, 57-58
Rightmire, George, 33, 72
Robinson, Frederick B., 25, 34, 40-41
Roosevelt, Eleanor, 62, 69, 90, 96-100, 102-103
Roosevelt, Franklin D., 14-15, 49, 62, 67, 69, 78, 80, 83-86, 90, 92, 96-99, 105
Ross, Irwin, 94
Rowell, Chester, 82
Russell, Charles E., 50
Ruthven, Alexander, 47
Ryan, George, 49

St. Joseph's College, 105
San Francisco *Chronicle,* 82
San Jose State College, 13, 16, 43
Sarah Lawrence College, 49, 65
Saturday Evening Post, 57
Schaflander, Gerald M., 6
Schrank, Charles, 21
Scottsboro boys, 75-76
Seeley, Evelyn, 27
Seidman, Harold, 57
Seldes, George, 55
Selective Service, 103
Sentries of American Youth, 46
Sinclair, Upton, 20, 31, 39
Smith College, 21, 36
Smith, Walter B., 22

Social Problems Club, Columbia University, 24, 76
Social Problems Club, University of California, Berkeley, 28
Socialist party, 87, 102, 105
Socialist Workers party, 89
Society for Student Liberties, 75
Southern California Student Conference Against War, 30
Southern Methodist University, 72
Spanish civil war, 78, 82-83, 86-87
Spectator, 11, 13, 22-23, 56, 58, 78-79, 81-82
Spivack, Robert, 83
Sproul, Robert G., 40, 52, 82
Stanford Daily, 8, 39
Stanford University, 16, 82
Stoner, Chance, 108
Strachey, John, 60
Strack, Celeste, 38, 40, 42, 79
Stroud, J. B., 14
Studebaker, John W., 62
Studenski, Paul, 10
Student, 25, 33
Student Advocate, 9, 57, 73, 79, 83, 108
Student Congress Against War, 30
Student League for Industrial Democracy, 20, 28, 32, 36, 38, 42, 46, 48, 56, 58, 61, 69-74, 76-77, 88, 93, 101
Student Outlook, 28-29, 42, 70-71, 100, 107
Student Outpost, 30, 45-46
Student Review, 26, 70, 75
Student Strike Against War, (1934) 37-38, 82, 107; (1935) 42-44, 56, 71, 82, 105; (1936) 52-53, 57, 78-79, 101, 104, 108; (1937) 78, 81-82
Supreme Court, 80
Susman, Warren L., 57, 60

Taft, Charles P., 94
Tansill, Charles C., 55
Taussig, Charles, 66
Texas A & M, 11
Thomas, Norman, 14, 32, 42, 52, 59, 70, 105, 107
Treaty of Versailles, 54
Tugwell, Rexford, 22, 26
Tulane University, 52

Union Theological Seminary, 21
United Mine Workers, 21
University of Arizona, 105

University of California, Berkeley, 5, 12, 19, 28, 31, 40, 42-43, 45-46, 52, 71, 81, 84, 87-88, 90, 105
University of California Board of Regents, 49
University of California, Los Angeles, 6, 30-31, 33, 35, 38-44, 53, 57, 64, 82, 106
University of Chicago, 12, 15, 22, 45, 50, 90
University of Colorado, 32, 106
University of Detroit, 7
University of Idaho, 11
University of Illinois, 44
University of Kansas, 66
University of Maine, 15
University of Maryland, 35
University of Michigan, 4, 9, 11, 14, 42, 47, 82
University of Minnesota, 42, 65, 74, 105
University of Missouri, 12, 16, 32
University of Nebraska, 32, 105
University of New Hampshire, 36
University of North Carolina, 20, 52
University of North Dakota, 63
University of Oklahoma, 38
University of Oregon, 11, 44, 71
University of Pennsylvania, 42
University of Pittsburgh, 46
University of South Carolina, 3
University of Southern California, 30, 75
University of Syracuse, 38
University of Texas, 12, 43, 52
University of Vermont, 3
University of Virginia, 108
University of Washington, 11, 15, 32, 52, 71, 75
University of Wisconsin, 5, 15, 33, 46, 50, 64
University of Wyoming, 7, 48

Vanderbilt University, 52
Vassar College, 37, 83, 86, 108
Veterans of Future Wars, 52-53
Virginia Union, 52

Wagner, Robert, 32
Walgreen, Charles, 50
Wallace, Henry, 62
Walsh, David, 66
Walters, Raymond, 63
Warner, Marie, 9
Washington State College, 51
Wayne University, 52
Wechsler, James, 43, 56, 58-60, 69, 95, 106-108
Weinstone, William, 76
Wesleyan University, 20
Western Washington College of Education, 27
Wheelock, John, 4
White, Elliott, 23
Wilkens, Ernest H., 47
Williams, Aubrey, 66, 84
Williams College, 4-5, 65
Wilson, Welford, 75
Wilson, Woodrow, 55
Wittner, Lawrence, 54
Works Progress Administration, 65, 74, 81
World Court, 66
World War I, 20, 54-55, 61, 64, 87, 94-95, 101, 107
World War II, 59, 90, 108
Wright, Roy, 76

Yale University, 3, 19, 27, 36, 40, 65
Yard, Molly, 83, 92
Yates, Dorothy, 13
Young Communist League, 46, 60, 76, 81, 84, 87
Young Men's Christian Association, 32, 67-68, 72, 81, 88
Young People's Socialist League, 87-88, 93
Young Women's Christian Association, 32
Youth Committee for the Oxford pledge, 86